The
networksage

We are pleased to share,
"The NetworkSage: Realize
Your Network Superpower,"
authored by our Advisor,
Dr. Glenna Crooks

Specializing in
3D Patient JourneySM

www.think-gen.com

Other Books

Covenants: Inspiring the Soul of Healing

Strategic Grantseeking for Community-Based Organizations

The
networksage

Realize Your Network Superpower

GLENNA CROOKS, PhD

THE NETWORKSAGE
REALIZE YOUR NETWORK SUPERPOWER

iUniverse books may be ordered through booksellers or by contacting:

iUniverse
1663 Liberty Drive
Bloomington, IN 47403
www.iuniverse.com
1-800-Authors (1-800-288-4677)

Because of the dynamic nature of the internet, any web addresses or links contained in this book may have changed since publication and may no longer be valid. The views expressed in this work are solely those of the author and do not necessarily reflect the views of the publisher, and the publisher hereby disclaims any responsibility for them.

Any people depicted in stock imagery provided by Thinkstock are models, and such images are being used for illustrative purposes only. Certain stock imagery © Thinkstock.

ISBN: 978-1-5320-2962-2 (sc)
ISBN: 978-1-5320-2963-9 (e)

Library of Congress Control Number: 2017915099

Printed in the USA.

iUniverse rev. date: 01/10/2018

any liability, loss, or risk, personal, business or otherwise, incurred as a consequence, directly or indirectly, from the use and application of the contents of this book.

Except for the author's own personal story, all names and identifying characteristics of individuals, families, or companies mentioned have been changed to protect their privacy.

To superheroes

especially

Mom and Dad

contents

Foreword

IN HER LATEST BOOK, *The NetworkSage: Realize Your Network Superpower*, Dr. Glenna Crooks describes automobile racing as a team sport. While the race car driver is the apparent hero on race day, the win depends at least as much on the efforts of a finely tuned, supportive pit crew.

Just so, she goes on to explain, our own success and the quality of our life experiences are dependent not only on our own efforts but also on the contributions of our own pit crews. She has immersed herself in the study of these pit crews for many years, realizing along the way they were networks. Glenna is a NetworkSage.

Each of us lives life supported by several network groups—a family network, a health and vitality network, a social and community network, and a career network, to name a few—and we are the pit crew in other people's networks as well.

In this book, we learn how to become aware of all the people in ours. We also learn the role that each of our networks and the players in them serves. In terms of action points, readers will learn the importance of structuring and managing networks for success, and they will get specific ideas about how to do so from people who have done it, succeeding in improving their health, personal relationships, family life, income, and careers and retirement and gaining peace of mind.

As a psychologist, most of my training focused on the study of the individual. How much more meaningful it is, as this book clearly elucidates, to think of individuals contextualized in terms of their networks, its players, and their interactions.

As the former CEO of a company with 250 employees, I believe I would have been far more effective in my job had I had the guidance of this book available to me at the time. It would have helped me to structure and manage the players in my business network far more effectively.

As a consultant in the health and wellness vertical, I firmly believe that one must become a NetworkSage to truly understand this field and its complexities. Issues like chronic disease management, patient drug adherence, or aging well, for example, can only be wrestled with meaningfully by taking the patient's networks into consideration.

Beyond health care, this book has other implications as well. Each of the eight networks Glenna describes has consequences for the health, happiness, success, and life satisfaction we all want for ourselves, our loved ones, and one another at every stage of life. It's time we take account of that.

Glenna has been one of my favorite thinkers and speakers. She got my attention years ago with a brilliant presentation about another one of her books, *Covenants: Inspiring the Soul of Healing*, and it changed my way of thinking. This book, I think, might well be the sequel to that one.

Bottom line. She's once again fundamentally changed my worldview in *The NetworkSage: Realize Your Network Superpower*. I'm betting something similar will happen to you too!

—Richard B. Vanderveer, PhD

preface

I LIKE ACTION MOVIES and superheroes. *Superman, Batman,* and *Jason Bourne* are thrilling, but *Iron Man* is my all-time favorite. An *Iron Man* marathon would be my idea of a great date night.

Iron Man had not yet been released in 2007, but I'd seen the trailer, so it's no surprise I noticed interviews with Robert Downey Jr. as they appeared on newsstands. I was already a fan.

Something he said at the time transformed my life. It was this: he had a "pit crew" of people helping him. In *W* magazine, he named a sensei, a psychiatrist, healing therapists, and his wife. In *Time* magazine, he mentioned his power-flow yoga teacher. His rationale for needing a pit crew? He was not a Model T, he explained, but a Ferrari, and it took a pit crew to keep him on the road.

First I reacted: *If you're a Ferrari, I'm at least a Maserati!*

Then I reflected: *You're right! Busy people do need support from others to travel the road of life!*

Next I wondered: *Who's in my pit crew?*

Eventually, I worried: *What about my family and friends? What about my clients? I'm in their pit crews! How well am I helping them navigate the busy lanes they travel?*

Some people say that "when the student is ready, the teacher appears," and that was the case for me. Mr. Downey Jr., brief as his comments were, piqued my curiosity. Then he taught me important lessons. He shifted my mind-set and showed me a new way of seeing life, one that fits today's complicated, fast-moving world. He shattered a long-held belief that I should be self-sufficient and independent, qualities I had been raised to value.

He was right; people need support from others, and lots of it, especially when they lead busy lives and have competing responsibilities in their families, careers, and communities. Support helps each of us individually and, in turn, helps all of us collectively. It was a big lesson. It made me think about my life differently, and my way of life changed because of it. Then others' lives changed too, and the NetworkSage road map emerged. In this book, you'll see how that happened.

An African proverb says, "If you want to go fast, go alone. If you want to go far, go together." Going together is how we live our lives as humans. We are, right from the start, social. The collective cooperation and interpersonal support we offer one another is the engine that drives humankind's progress and helps us live long, healthy, high-quality lives. How far you go—and I would argue how well and how fast—depends not only on you as an individual but on others too.

It is not solely your own health, education, and financial capital that determine your success. It is human capital too. In fact, more than any other resource at your disposal, human capital—yours and others'—will help you develop your talents, find your purpose, realize your potential, and achieve your dreams. Therein lies the superpower in your networks.

As your guide, I developed a road map you can follow and, better yet, one that you can adapt as you learn about it and use it to chart your own journey. It has six key features, and knowing about them in advance will provide you with signposts for what lies ahead. These include

1. my unshakable belief in your virtually unlimited human potential and the often underappreciated value of human capital;
2. our need, as humans, to connect with others and our human limits as we try, especially in an increasingly complicated world;
3. the imperative that you be in the driver's seat, not out of selfishness but born of your uniqueness as an individual and your place as connector-in-chief among all those in your networks;
4. the value of focusing on all your networks and the need for an organizing framework to do that well;
5. the importance of knowing how to ACTSage—that is being aware of your connections, having clarity about what you need and want from them, and using that information to transform your life to live better, healthier, happier, and more successfully in whatever you endeavor; and
6. the need for you and any road maps you use to be flexible and adapt to your circumstances and the world as both change.

This book addresses each one. Part 1 lays the groundwork, tells the story about how the journey began, and provides an overview of the key features of the NetworkSage road map that developed along the way. Part 2 describes the organizing framework of the networks that support you, the role each one plays, and ways you can explore yours. Part 3 describes the three ACTSage action steps that help you find and use network superpower. Part 4 brings the journey full circle, with reminders that not only do you rely on others but they rely on you and we all rely on one another.

Are you ready to begin? Would you like to go far *and* fast? Do you have big dreams? Are you building a legacy? Creating financial security for your family? Destined to be a leader in your community or professional field? Pushing beyond barriers of gender, gender identity, racial, ethnic, or disability that held you back to become a model of success for others? Hatching a big idea that will solve problems faced by humanity today? Providing care for a loved one? Building a new life for your three decades as a retiree? If so, you need to stay on track. Seeing life through the eyes of my favorite superhero gave me some ideas about pit crews—networks—and a NetworkSage road map that can help.

I'd like to know about your dreams, learn about your experiences, and hear about how you realized the superpower in your networks. Get in touch at www.sagemylife.com, and while you are there, look for additional stories, templates to help you gather and display network information, and resources for the journey ahead.

Key Points

- Human potential is virtually unlimited, and the value of human capital is underappreciated.
- As humans, we need to connect with others, yet there are limits to doing that well.
- You must be in the driver's seat, not out of selfishness but born of your uniqueness and your role as connector-in-chief.
- A network information architecture helps organize networks to help recall the people in them.
- ACTSage is a three-step process to become aware of your connections, gain clarity about your needs, and transform your networks.
- You and any road maps you use must be flexible and adapt to your circumstances and the world as both change.

introduction

IN 2007 WHEN ROBERT DOWNEY JR. talked about pit crews, I understood his reasoning. I needed a pit crew too. I had not been aware of how much, though, until his comments in those interviews. At the time, I had a suburban home with gardens I tended myself and was active in my church and community. I was founder and CEO of a global strategy firm working in public health. I did not have a family of my own, but I had been claimed by several as an adopted grandma, a role I loved. Young people sought me out as a mentor. Friends and clients sought me out as a confidante. Yes, I was busy, and I understood.

On Overload

In fact, I wasn't just busy. I was overloaded. It wasn't the first time, and I wasn't the only one who felt that way. Others I knew—teens, college students, stay-at-home moms, colleagues, and retirees—were busy and felt overloaded too. Everyone, it seemed, was balancing important family, friend, school, career, and community responsibilities.

If that sounds familiar, you know how being busy feels. You might also know how it feels when even being happily busy leads to overload. Perhaps this happened slowly as small, incremental household tasks, job assignments, friends' needs, or volunteer projects came your way. They didn't seem burdensome at first, but eventually they added up. Soon, your to-do list got far too long. Or perhaps it happened suddenly when life dealt you a wild card. It might have been a delightful wild card, by the way: a new relationship, a new baby, a new job, or a new retirement adventure. It might also have been a difficult one: a job loss, a serious illness, a caregiving crisis, or the death of a loved one.

Regardless of how it happens, overload has negative consequences. The stress of it triggers fight-or-flight reactions and leaves you with little time to pause, think well, sleep enough, or have fun. It gets in the way of your relationships, causing you to neglect those most important to you, including yourself and your needs. At times like that, it is tempting to work even harder and sleep even less to push through the obstacles. Do that for more than a very brief time, however, and you risk burnout. It is also tempting to deny the seriousness of the situation and hope troubles will magically disappear. Do that, and you can risk being unprepared for an even more troublesome outcome.

If this has happened to you even once, you know what comes next. You fall even further behind at work or at home or lose touch with family and friends. You are physically present but not emotionally available. You find it hard to distinguish between the important commitments you must keep and those you can renegotiate. You neglect your health and risk your job, your family's stability, and economic security. You feel frustrated and become angry easily. If you get to this point, you've run out of fuel, and when that happens, everyone suffers—especially you.

It's natural to be discouraged at times like that. It's common to feel abandoned and disconnected from others. It's possible to have an existential crisis and want to quit a job, sell a house (or build a tiny one), abandon responsibilities, and go off the grid. If you've ever felt that way, you're not alone. I know. I've been there myself, and others have confided in me that they have too. Though we may be tempted to cut and run, deep down we know that isn't what we really want. We love our families, our friends, and the people we serve through our careers. We want to make the world a better place. We have a sense of honor and want to keep the promises we've made. We don't want an escape route, just a better, wiser way to live.

And Underresourced

In the past, I believed overload was caused by some combination of big dreams and uncontrollable life circumstances. Now that I know about pit crews, I see the problem differently: the way we live our busy lives hasn't adapted to the reality of today's increasingly complex world and fragmented communities. Too many people are trying to do too much, too fast, and, worse yet, too alone. Are you one of them? I was.

Our ancestors lived in simpler times and could rely on support from nearby clans and villages. Today, we live in our 24/7/365 always-on world with smaller families, marital disruptions, and career mobility that take us far away from those traditional resources. In truth, you and I have alternative sources of support to replace those villages of old, but it was never obvious to me until that fateful day I was reminded of the vital role that pit crews play.

Help is all around; it's just hiding in plain sight. Pit crews are there at the ready. They can tow you out of a rut, lighten your load, and copilot as you navigate fast lanes. To engage their support, you need to be aware they exist, identify the people in them, know what you need from them, and ask for help. That wasn't something I knew was possible until 2007.

Why not? Perhaps it's American rugged individualism. Perhaps it is a mythic notion that "living independently" is the better way to avoid burdening others. Perhaps it is because losing a good grip on life's many moving parts happens too gradually to notice. That is, until one bad news story, text, or late-night phone call announces a problem that can't be ignored. For me, it is probably a bit of each of those reasons and more, as I've come to learn.

Now I know that being overloaded is hard, but being underresourced makes it worse. Without the support of close-by friends and family, big problems are devastating, and even small problems seem insurmountable. It takes a toll, one greater than most people ever know. How? Being chronically overloaded but underresourced harms the most precious resource available: you. It also harms another precious resource: the other people in your life. Times like that are ripe for losing a job, losing a lover, or losing self-respect. Those are expensive and sometimes unrecoverable losses and all because of the overloaded-but-underresourced dynamic that can overtake life.

Finding a Way Out

Sometimes the best way "out" is "through," and that is what I do in my day job. I am a strategist; I organize chaos and solve complex problems. The results are road maps people can use to put their drive and talent to work, and that is what I have done as a NetworkSage. This ability seems to come naturally, though my doctoral studies as an interdisciplinary social scientist certainly helped, giving me tools to solve problems others abandoned as hopeless. It's given me satisfying careers in education and in health care, in government, in a Fortune 50 company, as founder of a global strategy firm, cofounder of nonprofit organizations, and, most recently, founder of a technology company. I know people of all ages and from many nations, including US presidents, global company CEOs, and leaders in government, business, academia, and religion.

My work spans more than four decades, during which time I've usually been behind the scenes, except when on stage delivering speeches worldwide, sometimes on the topics of my books and often about the future. My approaches can be used in any sector, but my efforts have been devoted to education and public health. In schools, I developed programs to help children with special needs and talents and to help teachers feel more supported and satisfied in their careers. In public health, I focused on the special health concerns of men, women, children, seniors, and minorities. I've built policies and programs to help people with HIV/AIDS, hepatitis, stroke, chronic illness, rare diseases, Alzheimer's, cancer, diabetes, and intractable pain.

I won awards along the way, most recently being named a "2017

Disruptive Woman to Watch," but what I value more was the privilege of meeting and learning from extraordinary leaders. Maybe it's just my luck, but most of the people I meet, including the children, are on a quest to make this world a better place. As a confidential adviser, I got to know them personally. I am deeply honored they chose to share their deepest thoughts and feelings with me. I am in awe of them as they managed lives far more complicated and public than mine, with far more grace than I could have mustered had I been in their shoes.

Some of these extraordinary people were the product of privilege, with educational advantages and family connections that eased each step of the way. Others, me included, lacked social connections, were disadvantaged, and succeeded by dint of grit, determination, and the ability to recover from lessons learned in the school of hard knocks. People like that are inspiring, which makes seeing the barriers they face even more frustrating. Their hero's journey might seem romantic, but that is only the case in myth and fiction. For the real-life heroes I know, it has been tough, even for those from privileged circumstances. I often wish I could return and talk with them. I wish I could show them a better way. I wish I could tell them about pit crews.

A New Road Map

I can't go back in time, but I can go forward and teach what I've learned. This is an invitation for you to join me as I do. This book recounts the journey I embraced in earnest ten years ago, when a superhero sent me off without a map into unknown territory. I will show you how he changed my life and tell you about how it changed others' lives. I'll describe how I explored pit crews and, more importantly, how I came to see them as networks of people connected with each other as they connected with me. I'll explain why networks deserve far more attention than they receive and why networks are your superpower.

You'll meet parents who got a better education for a child with special needs, families and business owners who lowered their expenses and raised their income. You'll see how some people reconnected with their spirituality and how others went beyond typical work-life balance tensions to design creative, fluid adaptations to demanding careers and life circumstances. You'll meet people who restored their health and seniors well on their way to living independently, avoiding costly hospitalizations, assisted living, and institutional care.

Each person who embarked upon this journey had different life circumstances, but all of them faced challenges that are common today. Like me, they were overloaded and underresourced, facing complicated parenting, work, or aging situations. Like me, they lacked good road maps to guide them out of the chaos—and the fear— overtaking their lives. Sadly, they felt alone in their dilemmas. They didn't know that others, me included, faced similar struggles.

Like me, a few insights about pit crews, and they were off and running. Building good pit crews helped them redirect energy and talent to higher-impact, more satisfying activities. They had more time with loved ones and more success at work, and they made more productive, creative contributions to their communities. They had greater peace of mind. They live better, happier, healthier, more successful lives today because of my favorite superhero and his enlightening lesson about one of his superpowers: his pit crew.

How did it happen? The journey begins in the next chapter with the story about how a superhero rescued my busy life.

Key Points

- Busy people need support from others.
- Being overloaded places your valuable human capital at risk.
- Being underresourced as well risks harm to those you care for.
- Support to help you—pit crews—is there, hiding in plain sight.

part 1

SUPErHEroes and THE networksage road map

LIKE ALL SUPERHEROES STILL unaware they have superpowers, you have more potential than you know. As a NetworkSage, you will realize that potential. You can use this NetworkSage road map at every stage of life, alone or with trusted family, friends, or advisers. In fact, please reach out for help any time you feel the need. As a NetworkSage, you are surrounded by vast, often-untapped resources within your networks. They're your personal pit crew! Let them help!

By now, why I focus on pit crews—networks—may be obvious, but why *Sage*? A *sage* is one who becomes wise through experience and reflection. Drawing on the wisdom of the hundreds of people who have taken this journey, that is what this road map offers: a wiser way to live. I hope you will join us and become a NetworkSage too.

It is easy for me to encourage you. I've been informed by personal experience, but there are other considerations as well. Here are several: you are virtually guaranteed a much healthier and far longer life than those born just a century ago. You have access to better knowledge and tools than have ever been available. Your opportunities to explore— not only the outer-space heights of our galaxy but inner-space depths of our psyche—have never been greater. You are better equipped to find solutions to problems than any generation in history, which is a good thing given how many there are to solve.

When I wonder if humankind is up to modern-day challenges, I remember Roger Banister's four-minute mile. He accomplished the feat in 1954, when it was thought to be not only impossible but dangerous. Since then, each year, increasing numbers of people, some as young as high school, finish in even faster times. I believe that record-breaking trend in athletics applies to our intellectual ability, emotional intelligence, and moral capacity as well.

I see evidence of that in the people I know, and I invite you to watch for it in your own life. As we move forward into the future, the technology we develop will be *necessary*, but it will not be *sufficient*. Our very human challenges need what we, as humans, bring to the table. If you embrace this perspective and notice it on your journey, I believe you will share my optimism for the future and, no doubt, see new ways, as a NetworkSage, you can create it.

Chapter 1
Superhero to the Rescue

I DON'T SLOW DOWN. Ever. In fact, the Maserati analogy I mentioned earlier is a good one: it can travel at speeds of nearly two hundred miles per hour. As do I and just about everyone I know, multitasking all the while.

What keeps me going is my career. Oh, and family and friends and volunteer projects and gardening and hobbies. Get the picture? I love it all. Unfortunately, passion comes with a downside. Every few years, I take on too much. Convinced I have enough time and energy to do even more, I don't cut back on my schedule even when extra projects, unexpected travel, or snowstorms come my way. I fail to appreciate the difference between a Maserati and me. Well-engineered and well-maintained machines can perform at their peak for many years. That's not the case with people, regardless of how hard we try.

In 2007 when I saw the *Iron Man* trailer, I was headed toward overload once again. Many of my clients and friends were too. Although I encouraged them to ease up and get some rest, I was never that kind or wise with me. Instead, I'd blame myself, certain it was my fault. Clearly, I was doing something wrong—but what was it? Was I inefficient? Were my priorities all wrong? Did I need to be more resilient? Should I abandon my dreams?

Over the course of many decades, I found ways to recover at times like that and get back on track. I learned to live better doing *Seven Habits of Highly Effective People* with Steven Covey himself. Twice! I explored my limits rock climbing with Outward Bound. I improved my fitness hiking on the Appalachian Trail, taking active vacations, joining a gym, and hiring a trainer. To manage stress, I didn't just try yoga; I trained as a teacher, practiced mindfulness meditation, and occasionally talked with a therapist. To improve my company, I got a business coach.

I was a student of anything that would help me when overload got the upper hand. Each technique worked, by the way. Each one restored my health, improved my mood, and refueled me for the road ahead. I recommitted to my life's work and became ever more productive and even more satisfied. Then, before long, the cycle would start all over again. I'd get overloaded, crash, and recover.

What was I doing wrong?

Working at the Edge

Eventually, it dawned on me that I'd been watching this pattern unfold for decades and not only in me. I'd seen it in friends and colleagues, in local communities, and on the global stage. No one was immune, but people deeply committed to transforming the world—as parents, on the job, or in the community—seemed particularly at risk. It happened to both men and women, but women seemed more vulnerable. Working women with a "second shift" at home caring for children or with a "third shift" caring for elderly parents or in-laws were especially vulnerable. We were living on an edge and not doing it very well.

Worse yet, it wasn't only that we lived this pattern of overload-crash-and-recovery but that each time we did, it became progressively harder to recover and reengage. We all felt that life was getting tougher, and some of us worried we were not tough enough to cross the finish line. Was that just the increasing complexity of the world? Could we succeed in the multiple roles we played, or was that an impossible dream? Could we be parents, advocates for children with special needs, adult children of elderly parents, intimate partners, helpful friends, managers, and engaged community volunteers? Could anyone? Many of us were working at the edge of our capacity, and someone needed to pull us back from the brink. But who?

It worried me when people thought their only way out was to quit. They were friends. I didn't want them to end a career feeling like failures. Overload was forcing them into an early retirement, and that placed their financial future at risk. They were also colleagues. I knew the impact of losing their talent to the workforce. They were solving important public health, national security, and economic growth problems. The world needed all hands on deck. I didn't want them to give up yet. Or ever! I wanted to pull them back before they went over the edge. But how?

Finally, after one too many late nights listening to talented people say they wanted to bail out, I engaged a colleague and friend, Jonathan Peck, president of the Institute for Alternative Futures, to find a way to help. We designed a one-day experience we called Best Edge, during which the two of us met with one person to create a one-year strategic plan for his or her life. Strategic plans helped our organizations thrive, and we felt they could help individual people too. We guessed right. During that day of brainstorming, we addressed every aspect of their personal, family, caregiving, and work life. We found ways to combine the things they needed to do with what they wanted to do so they could be more efficient. We noticed gaps, especially in self-care, exercise, or fun, and explored ways to add those.

It worked. I'm pleased to say that not one person who started the day saying they wanted to leave a job, a marriage, or both did so. In fact, they went on to even happier lives and greater accomplishments. They stepped back from the brink.

Unfortunately, Jonathan and I had other businesses to run, and this one-day event was not scalable. I wanted to help more people and went looking for an alternative. When I heard about pit crews, I wondered if that might be the route to take.

Pit Crew Test Drive

I had explored pit crews already but without realizing it. Several years earlier, a business coach suggested I make a list of everyone I managed as a business owner. In all, that list included 150 people. Mine was a niche firm, so only a small number were employees. Others on the list included an accountant, attorney and IT support. The largest group included clients, their bosses, staff, and customers. I hadn't viewed those 150 people as a pit crew, but they were. They were my business pit crew. They kept my business running well.

Creating that list made me aware of my management load for the first time. It helped me gain clarity about the characteristics of an ideal employee, ideal vendor, and ideal client. It showed me ways to transform my business operations. I didn't call it ACTSage yet, nor did I rigorously apply network insight. I didn't have any at that point. Nonetheless, it made my business run better, especially when I learned that, as "knowledge workers" managing complex problems and sometimes high-conflict situations, we needed more downtime. We cut back to a four-day workweek; our productivity and income skyrocketed.

Despite the success of that business-life exercise, I didn't think to do something similar in my personal life. The 2007 aha moment about pit crews spurred me to try. I didn't do this in one sitting, by the way. I kept notes on the kitchen counter, adding names over the course of several weeks as people came to mind. Sometimes this happened because I saw them on weekend errands. Or a bill would arrive, and that would remind me. I scanned my Outlook contacts to find others. The list included friends and family, my physician and dentist, dry cleaners, community groups, and people who helped maintain and improve my home. I thought I was done and stopped.

	My List	
	Acupuncturist	Financial Planner
	Dentist	Education Volunteer Project Committee - 4
	Pilates Instructor	Child Health Volunteer Project Board - 15
	DB	NHZ
	Skin care	MEH
○	Hungry ghost - ALC	Hair Colorist
	Friendly ghost – Grandpa	Hungry ghost – Elementary School Teachers - 6
	Hair Stylist	Tailor
	Brother and Sister-in-Law	Friendly ghost – Girl Scout Leaders – 2
	Niece – JC	Internist
	Niece – DC	OB-GYN
	Mom	Snow removal
	Dad	Home Inspector
	LMF	Plumber
	Priest	Electrician
	Psychiatrist	Roofer
○	Accountant	Image consultant
	Landscape Installer	Yoga Instructor
	Dry Cleaners	Manicurist
	Pharmacist	Volunteer Project - 4
	Optometrist	Volunteer Project - 5
	JLK	Prayer Group - 12
	Attorney	Internist Office Staff - 3
	Banker	OB-GYN Office Staff -3
	Insurance Agent	Security Alarm Company
	Assistant Priest	Auto Dealer Service Department – Tony
	Carpenter	Septic System Cleaner
	House cleaner	Massage Therapist
	Landscape Designer	Dental Assistant/Hygienist
○	Landscape Care/Grass Cutting	Optometrist Office Staff -1
	Tree Care	Paternal Cousins – 7
	Friendly ghost – NNM	Maternal Cousins – 27
	Family – Maternal Uncle	Friendly Ghost – Paternal Aunt
	Family – Maternal Aunt	Friendly Ghost – Paternal Uncle
	Hungry Ghost – HS Guidance Counselor	Friendly Ghost – Best Friend's Mom
	Integral Coach	Hungry Ghost – Maternal Uncle
	JJM	

As I've learned since, no list like this is ever complete. Life changes, and when it does, our business- and personal-life pit crews change too. New people arrive because we invite them in. Or our business or personal life changes, and they invite themselves. Some people leave, either because we ask them, they decide for themselves, or our life paths diverge. Eventually, I understood my list would never be finished and didn't need to be perfect. It just needed to be good enough to help me manage for the foreseeable future. My good-enough personal pit crew list? It was 139 people long. That was what it took to keep just me and my household going: 139 people.

Am I high maintenance or what?

I had no complaints about the 150 people on my business pit crew list. I had great clients, good technology, and management systems to keep it all in order. I did, however, feel plenty of angst about the size of my personal pit crew. I complained to friends but got no sympathy. They thought I was lucky to have so many people helping me out. Quite the contrary, I didn't feel lucky, and the list didn't feel good.

Creating the list reminded me of how worn down I was by fifteen phone calls to coordinate schedules with a plumber and an electrician to discuss a simple home improvement. I recalled the time I waited three hours in a physician's office despite careful planning to be the day's first appointment. It showed me all the people required to maintain my home. It reminded me of friends in western time zones who called late at night though they knew my East Coast day starts very early. No wonder I felt worn down. Those good business management practices? They didn't work in my personal life.

Eventually, I stopped complaining, realizing that mine was a comparatively simple life. I didn't have a spouse, so there were no in-laws or spouse's colleagues or friends on my list. I didn't have children or stepchildren, so I wasn't engaging playgroups, teachers, doctors, orthodontists, or coaches on their behalf. My elderly mom was healthy, living independently, and didn't need my caregiving support. I was healthy and didn't need specialist doctors. My friends weren't facing crises either. I didn't have a dog. Or a cat! Work kept me busy, but everyone else I knew was busy with work too. Compared to others, my life was simple, and my pit crew was streamlined.

Mind Shifting

Streamlined or not, I needed a pit crew that worked for me. My complaints were real, but they were vague. I set about to gain clarity, which came when I paid more attention to each person, making notes on the list along the way.

I saw that some people were helpful, but not everyone was. Some were fun to be with; others not so much. Some were skilled, and others less so. Some enriched my life, but not everyone did. Some were proactive and managed me; others needed reminders to meet the deadlines they promised. Some anticipated my needs; others couldn't comply with a simple request. Some were very important to me, but not everyone was. What's more, those who were important were important for different reasons.

Regardless, all of them needed attention. That took time and energy and sometimes created wear and tear on me. Gradually, my thinking about my life and pit crews evolved in important ways.

I Need a Pit Crew

My life may have been simple compared to others, but to me it seemed complicated, and mismanagement wasn't an option. Like any homeowner, for example, mine was a major investment; I could not afford the financial loss if it fell into disrepair. My work and international travel were demanding; I could not risk the consequences of missing a speech or making a mistake. I made commitments to friends and in my community and wanted to keep those promises.

I did what I could to keep my life in good working order, staying organized, healthy, and fit, and those were *necessary*. They were not *sufficient*, however, to prevent my becoming overloaded. Even on the best days, I need a pit crew.

I Need a Good Pit Crew

Not only did I need a pit crew, I needed a good pit crew that could go the distance! Life wasn't a quarter-mile drag race; it was an endurance run longer than any automotive team would attempt. It wasn't a sprint or even a marathon. In fact, it was longer than even an ultramarathon. It wasn't wise to continue the cycle of overload-crash-and-recovery; prevention was the better way, and a good pit crew would help.

Pit Crews Are Networks

Before long, it was clear the individuals on my list rarely worked in isolation from one another. In many cases, they were connecting with one another as they were connecting with me. These were networks! Every encounter we had—positive or negative—could reverberate throughout our shared connections and beyond.

Sometimes these networks worked well, like when a neighbor's friend from church became the contractor who managed a renovation project. Long after the job was done, his crew was a reliable source of handyman help. They saved me the time and energy of searching for others and prevented mistakes caused by hiring the wrong people. He even showed up in the middle of a hurricane when my sump pump broke, bringing me one of his own to prevent storm damage to my home.

Sometimes, however, it didn't work well, like when I blew off some steam during a stressful week and confided in someone who later proved untrustworthy. That momentary loss of self-control and lapse in judgment echoed throughout networks that mattered. The repair work took energy that I'd rather have spent elsewhere.

I Am on Pit Crews

Finally came an important aha moment: I was on other people's pit crews! I cared deeply for my family, friends, and clients. I was engaged in volunteer activities that I valued. This led me to wonder if

I supported others well enough. I never had the courage to ask, but I knew there were times I didn't. In retrospect, most of those times had something in common: I let others down when I was overloaded or embroiled in a crisis because my own pit crews failed to support me or, worse, created additional burdens on me.

That was a radicalizing insight. My pit crews needed to support me not just for selfish reasons as I lived my own life but because I supported others! I didn't just need a pit crew! I was *on* pit crews! I could not be a good daughter, sister, aunt, friend, neighbor, mentor, adviser, strategist, problem solver, CEO, or adopted grandma without help. My productivity, business brand, personal reputation, sense of caring, and personal honor were at stake. Yes, it was time to make some changes.

Time for a Tune-Up

To my surprise, making changes was easier than expected, especially in the beginning. Perhaps that is because, as a busy person, I had time to focus only on the small ones. As I learned later, however, and as you'll soon see from stories about others, minor changes are the butterfly effects that catalyze truly transformative life change.

I began by simplifying my life. After a lifetime of doing my own housework and errands, I decided it was time to get help. I sorted my list into two sections: those that required my personal attention and those that did not. Then I created a job description and hired a local community college student for just a few hours each week to manage all the people and tasks that did not require my personal attention. That eliminated interactions with lots of clerks. Eventually, she took on other tasks, like ordering, wrapping, and mailing gifts for birthdays and holidays. Occasionally, she'd surprise me with dinner when I got home late from an out-of-town trip. It didn't take long to learn the value of her help. She didn't just save me time; she saved me wear-and-tear weariness that I didn't realize was draining me until I had energy to spare.

Next, I made my life easier by replacing high-maintenance people who were wearing me down. Doing this meant I needed additional clarity about what I wanted from others, and though that might sound obvious, it's not something I'd done before. It was at this point I realized how much I valued my time, for example. For that reason, when I show up on time for services that require appointments, I am willing to wait but not for long. The hairdresser who always kept me waiting at least an hour (and once nearly caused me to miss a flight!) was the first to go. Rather than making the effort to find another convenient appointment time with the physician who kept me waiting for three hours, I found another doctor.

I also came to appreciate the value of the peace of mind I have when my affairs are in order. For that reason, when I engage experts to help, I expect them to do the job correctly by the deadlines they agreed to meet. At the time, I had been increasingly dissatisfied with my attorney and accountant but dreaded the time-consuming effort to find new ones and make the switch. The clarity I gained at this point made the decision easier. It helped me see the drain on me caused by not having an up-to-date last will and living will, the frustration of missed deadlines, and the weariness of excuses about how commitments to other clients got in the way of commitments to me.

As for the friends in other time zones who called me late at night, I knew their lives were busy and they might forget my day starts much earlier than theirs. To put an end to those late-night calls, I borrowed an idea from a client who traveled far more often than me; I set a boundary by turning off the phone as I headed for bed each night.

Even those few simple steps improved my quality of life almost overnight. I had more time to be creative and spend in the garden, which is where I did my best thinking. My health and mood improved. I had more energy for friends, family, and the career I loved. I did preventive maintenance projects at home. I (finally!) had the energy to tackle important but unpleasant file-organizing projects that had often been rescheduled for "sometime next week."

Shifting into Higher Gear

For several years, my efforts were personal. All I wanted was good support from people on my list to make my life easier. Creating a good pit crew helped. Eventually, others noticed the change in me and wanted to know my secret. Those who embraced even my very earliest and still-evolving insights about networks enjoyed their own version of success. I was glad when my life improved and even more delighted when others experienced similar results. Before long, they were teaching me what they learned, and with their encouragement, I committed to this journey to explore networks and build a road map.

As time passed, I learned that good networks did more than make life easier. Networks helped to unleash pent-up human potential. It wasn't obvious at first, but eventually it was crystal clear: being sage in *any* part of life enabled success in *every* part of life. In my case, the help of someone to manage weekend errands rippled through every other day. That was true for others too. They saw barriers fall away and benefits ripple throughout their networks and across multiple generations of their families. Building good pit crews helped redirect energy and talent to higher-impact, more satisfying activities. Everyone had more time with loved ones and more success at work. They made more productive, creative contributions to their communities. Best of all, they had greater peace of mind.

Watching this happen reminded me why Jonathan and I had created Best Edge in the first place and then why I explored the idea of pit crews afterward. It wasn't just to make life easy. It was to find a way to help talented people who stood at the brink, questioning life, doubting their ability to succeed, and wondering if they should quit.

With ever-growing insights about networks, I could see that my clients were not just exhausted from overload. Regardless of their willingness to work hard and their fearlessness in the face of adversity, they were underresourced as well. Like me, some of them lacked adequate support networks. Others had robust networks but didn't manage them well. And to top it off, none of us had a NetworkSage road map (yet!) to follow. Those observations were at odds with two long-held beliefs, and the disconnection between what I *experienced* and what I *believed* spurred my commitment to help people stay in the race and win. Those two beliefs?

First, human potential is vast, and we are far from reaching its limit. Even under adverse conditions, people can accomplish great things, and given the right conditions, people can flourish even more. Second, human capital is our highest-value asset. Developing human capacity and investing in human capital pays rich dividends. Those beliefs were formed decades before, watching my parents navigate their life circumstances.

Lessons Learned

My parents' families did not recover from the losses suffered from the Great Depression and Second World War. It was especially difficult for my mom's family, since her father died when she was young, leaving her mother to raise six children alone. Their families could not launch them into adult life with the resources to make success a certainty and life easier. Their lack of educational, economic, and social advantages made us, at best, among the working poor. We lived in the Chicago area in a too-small home, and they drove an old car with floorboards so rusted out we could see the street below. There was always enough food in the pantry to make it to payday, though rarely enough to make it one day more. We did not take vacations. Treats—or a dime to swim at a public pool—were rare.

When I was in fourth grade, my parents created a plan to improve our family's chances for a better life. They passed on a store-clerk job opportunity for Mom in favor of an alternative, longer-term journey. Making investment-and-return calculations worthy of any finance major, they built a seven-year road map: Mom would start college and earn a bachelor's degree to become a teacher. It would take that long because she could attend classes only part-time. After all, she had three children, we had only that one old car, and her college was in another city, a three-hour round-trip bus ride, with transfers along way.

This was long before it was fashionable for mothers to start—or return—to college and meant bucking the prevailing views about a woman's role in the world. Nonetheless, they set off on this journey, though their families criticized the plan, worrying often and aloud that my brothers and I would be neglected and become delinquents. (We weren't, and we didn't.) On the contrary, we all pitched in, and as kids, we acquired valuable life skills. We learned to grocery shop and do yard work and household chores. I learned to sew my own clothes, and though I'm a good cook, my brothers are even better.

When I was in seventh grade, just three nights before Christmas and one day before Mom's sophomore finals, Dad was seriously injured while working at his job on the railroad. What followed were several surgeries, the first one the next morning. As the oldest child, I managed things at home, finished wrapping presents, and prepared for the holiday. Mom went to the hospital, and when Dad was safely out of surgery, she drove to campus and took her tests. We visited him at the hospital on Christmas Eve. It would take nearly two years for Dad to recover, during which time meager union and work-related benefits ran out. There was virtually no money, save loans from one family member, which came with doses of shame heaped upon my parents and spilt over onto us kids.

Now living well below the poverty line, my parents responded with even more belt tightening. We got our food from day-old bread stores and warehouses that sold damaged canned goods and overripe fruits and vegetables. Dad cut my brothers' hair, and I learned to cut my mom's and my own. Babysitting money helped me afford some school and Girl Scout activities, and my brothers had paper routes, grass-cutting, and snow-shoveling jobs. At this point, my parents made an even tougher investment decision. Though their families continued to criticize, rather than abandon their plan, they shifted gears and accelerated it: Mom got school loans, studied year-round, and took more than a full load of classes.

Mom graduated with honors. Before the ink was dry on her diploma, she landed a teaching job at her childhood elementary school, located in what was now the highest-poverty, sometimes-dangerous area of our city. That's when she learned for the first time that, though she needed a bachelor's degree to get her job, she needed a master's degree to keep it. Once again, they rose to the challenge. Rather than seeing this as a setback and to avoid losing momentum, she pressed on, teaching during the day and taking classes at night and during summers.

Eventually, and in less time than their initial plan, my mom and dad accomplished more than their dream. Not only did Mom have a bachelor's degree; she had a master's as well. Even the adversity of Dad's accident, as difficult as it was during his recovery, didn't keep them from success. As an unexpected bonus, we got an instant replay of each day's lectures during dinner. Also as a bonus, her master's degree program required she spend a summer at the university's main campus, a four-hour drive from home. As a junior in high school, I was admitted to Indiana University and spent the summer on the Bloomington campus with her, taking classes that counted toward my degree.

Their very hard work and difficult investment decisions eventually paid off. Over the next several decades, they could afford a better car, move to a better neighborhood, buy a small vacation cottage on a nearby lake, and retire comfortably. Better times did not happen soon enough to help me though. Just two weeks after Mom finished her master's degree, I was scheduled to start college as a freshman. At the time, we were still living a near-poverty lifestyle. Though both Mom and Dad were working, they still had family, bank, and her school loans to pay and could not afford to cover all my costs as they had hoped. They could help but not enough. Because their debt load was not factored into the college's financial-need calculations, I did not qualify for low-income student grants. For months, it appeared that I would not be able to start IU on time.

Road Maps Followed

I made it through college because of how well I'd absorbed my parents' values and learned their road map to reach a dream: plan, invest in yourself, work hard, and take informed risks. Their success fueled my willingness to follow their lead and give it a try. Making careful financial and course requirement plans, I went to school year-round. I worked two part-time jobs (one around food to be sure I could eat) and got loans. Just as my mom and dad accomplished more than their dream, I did too, completing bachelor's and master's degrees in four years. Joining the workforce earlier than planned gave me an extra year's salary that more than justified my debt load. A few years later—fully aware of the opportunity cost involved—I left my job to earn a doctorate, forgoing income for nearly three years. That paid off too.

This road map didn't dead-end with a PhD. Leaving the Midwest to relocate to Washington without a job in hand was difficult and risky but paid off with an appointment by President Ronald Reagan to a post in his administration. It was the best postdoc anyone ever did. Years later, given the choice between remaining in Washington and relocating for a job in another state, I accepted the offer to work for the Most Admired Corporation in America. That move was even more difficult, but I learned from the best colleagues in the health care sector, and it pays dividends yet today. Pursuing enrichment programs through the Covey Leadership Center, Ken Wilber's Integral Institute, and Zen Master Genpo Roshi's BigMind did too. Investing in my health and in my business paid off. Connecting with people who were smarter and wiser—and mentoring those who turned to me—taught me more than any classroom lecture.

Hidden Assets Revealed

Yes, human capital—mine and others'—has always been my most-valued, highest-return asset, though I wasn't consciously aware of it at the time. Only in retrospect did I see that investing in myself and connecting with others produced far greater gains than any investment I made in home ownership or a 401(k). And they were far more secure and stable than housing-market bubbles and Wall Street market corrections.

If human capital is my highest-value asset, why did I place it at such great risk for so many years with unhealthy cycles of overload and burnout? Why didn't I nurture the asset so important to every aspect of my life? Why hadn't I engaged pit crews to help me?

Some people say, "It takes a village ..." and my parents had one: family, friends, neighbors, church, their children's school, Mom's college, and Dad's workplace. Even though during their worst times my parents never abandoned others, very few people in their village showed up to help them. Work benefits ran out quickly. Family handouts came with the burden of shame and disapproval that haunt us to this very day. Neighbors, friends, and those at church and our school didn't reach out, even to offer encouragement.

Why no village safety net arrived to help remains a mystery to me. In contrast, it is no mystery why I will never forget what Robert Downey Jr. said in 2007. Had a village come to our aid and made it easier for us, I might not have noticed his quip about pit crews. His few words might not have shattered the limiting mind-set created during those childhood years. They would not have catalyzed the radical mind shift that has transformed my life and the lives of others today. Without him, I would not have known I needed to unlearn some childhood lessons.

My parents climbed out of poverty and survived the extended period of Dad's recovery not *because* of their village but *despite* it. They define grit. Their experience taught me two hard lessons, and the first one was good: getting ahead means planning, investing, taking informed risks, working hard, sacrificing, and delaying gratification. That lesson served me well. It encouraged me to invest in my education and kept me in school—especially during doctoral studies—when nearly everyone else dropped out. It has played an important role in much of what I've done since. It shaped my views about the human potential to succeed, even under adverse conditions, and it strengthened my optimism about humanity's future.

Unfortunately, the second lesson has been hard to unlearn: achieving one's potential means going it alone on an uphill road of limiting biases. With no early-life example to draw upon, it never occurred to me that I could engage others to help. I never imagined that I could even find cheerleaders to encourage me through tough times. Since I never heard my parents complain about the criticism and lack of support they received—not even once—I took for granted that life was that way for everyone. I assumed that the weariness and limits I felt were personal failings and never imagined my own networks might also be responsible.

I'm still unlearning this last lesson. Today, though, I can say that childhood experiences I would never have wished on anyone, with the help of a superhero, may eventually help everyone. What he taught me resonates with what I learned while pulling weeds with my dad as we listened to the Indy 500 race on the radio, and it rings true now more than ever. It's this: regardless of a driver's skill and a car's engineering excellence, on race day, success depends heavily on the support of a good pit crew. As drama unfolds on the racecourse, it can be easy to ignore what a pit crew does. Racing experts, however, don't. They know that a race can be won or lost in the pit. My favorite superhero had it right. He needs support from other people. So do I. So do you.

Key Points

- Human potential is nearly unlimited.

- Human capital—yours and others'—is your highest-value asset.
- Networks of people support every aspect of your life, not just your career.
- You are in others' networks, supporting them. To do it well, you need support.

Chapter 2
Connections Fuel Your Future

ARE YOU READY FOR the road that lies ahead? It's certain to be a long one. What will you do with the three decades of longer, healthier life span than those born just a century ago? How do you envision the years you have been given to raise your family, build your career, contribute to your community, and enjoy retirement? As you look ahead, is the future you envision one you hope for? Or is it one you fear?

If it's a future you hope for, one where daydreams come true, you may need to take steps to assure they do. If it's a future you fear, one where nightmares become real, you may need to prepare, and perhaps prevent the harm they could otherwise cause.

The NetworkSage journey has taught me and others that, whatever the future, having the right people around every step of the way is essential. Doing that will be easier if you understand three things about the human capital available to help you prosper: first, the realities and risks of your social nature; second, the social complexity of your modern life; and third, the limits of our shared human—and your personal—capacity to manage connections with others.

Your Social Nature

You are social by nature, and even as a mature, resourceful adult, you can't live alone for long. Stories of hermits living in isolation are just that—stories. In truth, hermits lived near other hermits and close to towns. Each may have led more solitary lives than others of their time and place, but they were not alone. In fact, they were frequently sought out for the counsel they provided and the healing arts they knew.

Eighty percent of your waking time is spent with others, and being with them helps you as they share knowledge, skills, work, and resources. In the past—and even for very young children today—that knowledge may have been as basic as which foods were safe to eat and why it was important to avoid fire. Hunting and farming skills essential to your ancestors' survival were shared with younger people. We do likewise when we teach study skills and social graces to prepare children for school exams and the emotional quotient (EQ) they need for twenty-first-century jobs. Now as then, family units, friends, and neighbors share work. Couples divide workloads. Parents assign chores to children. Generations of family members help one another. Friends help friends. Neighbors raise barns, have block parties, and hold yard sales. Work teams collaborate to assure project success and business growth.

Good Connections Help

As a child, having others around, especially close kin, improved your chances of surviving to adulthood. That's not just the case for ancient times; it's still true today. Even in the developed world, a study published in the journal *Evolution and Human Behavior* showed that the presence of other kin, especially a maternal grandmother, improves the chances a child will survive. When a child survives, it improves the chances that the kin group and the larger group they belong to will survive as well. There is more to life than survival, though.

Living with others fills social needs, and those are not trivial. You need support, understanding, humor, gossip, respect, and appreciation. These are essential to being human. You need people to celebrate with you when times are good and comfort you when times are not. Carlin Flora describes the need for good connections well in *Friendfluence: The Surprising Way Friends Make Us Who We Are*, and each week, it seems, new insights about the importance of our social nature emerge from a variety of scientific fields.

Good connections are good for your health, for example. They make you more resilient in stressful times and even ease physical pain. They help you remain in your community as you age, living healthy. A good connection with someone releases the hormone oxytocin, reducing anxiety. This happens not only when others do something good for you but also when you do something good for others. This may be why, of all the exercises tested by educator and positive-psychology author Martin Seligman, doing a kindness for another produced the most reliable increase in a person's own well-being.

Good connections in a good social sphere benefit you economically. If your friends, family, and teachers set high expectations for your educational and career success, in both subtle and direct ways, that helped you to reach those targets. Good connections help you share risks, get emergency help, borrow money, find mates, and get jobs, not just because your friends have resources but also because your friends know people that you don't. The people in our friends' networks, including those you may not know because they are friends of friends, for example, are the principal source of information about new jobs and prospective mates. Good social connections at work can help you cope with pay cuts, fewer work hours, and other benefit losses during economic downturns, according to a study published in the *Journal of Occupational and Organizational Psychology*.

Bad Connections Harm

As you might expect, bad connections have negative consequences. People in poor-quality marriages are more likely to suffer from hypertension and have lower rates of survival following a heart attack. Even young people (between the ages of eighteen and fifty-five) who have heart attacks have poorer outcomes when they lack good social support. Being disconnected is also bad for your health. This is one of the consequences of hypermobility caused by extensive work-related travel; it breaks down family and social relationships that support health.

In your community, if connections with your friends and family are not good or all of you are confined in a bad neighborhood, studies show that can work against you. If your children attend school in a run-down building with leaking toilets, broken furniture, and smelly cafeterias, they'll be more likely to get lower grades. If they attend school in a disadvantaged district with more minority students, they are less likely to receive accommodations for their disabilities and more likely to be punished for talking back and classroom disruptions. If your neighborhood is unsafe, it is not even necessary for you to be a victim of violence to feel the impact. Teens who feel unsafe are more likely to be depressed, be aggressive, and achieve less academically. Older people in those neighborhoods are less likely to take walks, an important exercise to maintain their weight, mood, social engagement, and health.

If your connections have low aspirations, yours can suffer. If they have not achieved educational success, a college education, or a job, it will be more difficult for you to do so. You will be less likely to have someone to help you make connections, improve your life circumstances, or rely on in a crisis. Worse, the effects of living in a poor neighborhood continue. Breaking free of poverty is good for you and future generations, but if you succeed, as a study published in the *Journal of Youth and Adolescence* indicates, the combined stress of living in adversity and striving to change can cause irreversible negative health effects in your adult years.

Loneliness Hurts

Worse than a bad connection is being shunned by others altogether. If you feel lonely, rejected, or neglected by family or friends—John Cacioppo, director of the University of Chicago's Center for Cognitive and Social Neuroscience, says 26 percent of Americans do—those are not only painful feelings but risk factors for disease. Rates of loneliness in older people, as shown by a University of California-San Francisco study, are even higher: 43 percent. Disturbingly, both statistics exceed rates of loneliness in the 1970s when, as Cacioppo notes, they were 11 percent.

This is important because medical studies have shown that loneliness and lack of social connections are more harmful to your health than smoking, obesity, or alcoholism. They increase infections, depression, and cognitive decline. They interfere with sleep and increase blood pressure and stress hormones. Even the symptoms of a common cold feel worse if you are lonely, according to research by Rice University psychologist Chris Fagundes and his colleagues. Loneliness even has an impact at a cellular level, changing gene expression in immune cells. It is a predictor of depression, chronic illness, and shorter life span. If you've ever experienced social pain—from isolation, rejection, or loneliness—recent neuroscience studies have shown it not only *feels* like real pain but *is* real pain and travels along the same neural pathways as physical pain. "Sticks and stones may break my bones, but words will never hurt me" is a child's rhyme, not a human truth. Social isolation, rejection, and loneliness hurt.

Connections Influence

Network connections also influence your behavior. Even if you don't drink alcohol and eat snacks now, if you have friends, family, or a spouse who do, you'll be more likely to do so eventually. If you are an older person whose spouse is frail or depressed, you are more likely to become frail or depressed yourself. If you are a college student who observes a friend texting while driving, you'll be more likely to do the same.

Social connectedness is so powerful that the people you know *and* the people they know that you do not know have an impact on you through a kind of "social contagion." Social distance does not insulate you. Yale sociologist and physician Nicholas Christakis captivated audiences with his TED Talks on the subject. His research on how obesity spreads through social networks tells a compelling story. If you have an obese friend, for example, you are at a 57 percent increased chance of being obese eventually. That risk increases to 71 percent if the friend is the same sex. If you and your friend have mutual friends, the risk increases to 171 percent. Depression in your friend's friends' friends (that is, people who are friends of friends of friends that you don't know) can contribute to your mood, especially if they are women. That's right. You need not even *know* people socially distant from you to experience the impact of their moods or behaviors on yours. As noted by Brian Wansink in *Slim by Design: Mindless Eating Solutions for Everyday Life*, even the behavior of a stranger can influence yours. His studies showed that when eating near an overweight stranger, people tend to eat unhealthier foods.

What does all this mean and how can we possibly know the friends of our friends of our friends? In my experience, it is possible to explore socially distant connections; just ask! Most people, however, are not even *aware* of their own, direct, first-degree connections. I wasn't when I began this journey, and that's the place to start. Then, if you are like me and curious about how a much broader network of friends of friends might impact you today or in the future, you can ask your friends about their friends. I know from experience, however, that even if you choose to focus only on connections in your own network home, it will be worth the time, and you will reap great benefits.

Even when those around you are supportive, can you have too much of a good thing? I believe the answer to that is yes. What is the risk? Your future and all your goals, because the world today is more socially complex than ever and there are limits to managing connections well.

Modern-Day Social Complexity

Some scholars say life today is far more stressful and demanding than in times past. As a social scientist, I would agree, especially in relation to our social nature and needs. Compare then to now. Your ancestors lived in small gatherings of clans, hunted in small bands, and camped overnight in small groups. Even as recently as several generations ago, they were surrounded by people who were a lot like them in culture, language, history, religious belief, and tradition. Towns were small by today's standards. People attended school, church, and festivals with other people they knew. Those repeated, spontaneous contacts were a key ingredient in forming friend and neighborhood bonds. Marriages ended by death, not by divorce and remarriage.

Your long-ago ancestors rarely needed specialists. Doctors and midwives? For certain. Accountants? Probably not. Attorneys? Rarely. Only relatively recently did education become universal, so many never even learned to read. They had little contact with the world beyond their town, which was walled to keep everyone safe. Although they welcomed traders, strangers also came as conquerors, so they were suspicious of anyone they did not know until they could sort friend from foe. News traveled but only as fast as foot traffic, horseback, or caravan could carry it. Productive work ended at nightfall.

Compare that to your life today. Your village is global. Your city, state, and national borders are open. News is instantaneous, and communication technologies and lights are always on. You need specialists to help you manage your marital status, health, educational progress, financial and legal affairs, and household and work obligations. Time with friends is rarely spontaneous; it requires planning.

Your most adventurous ancestors may have been pioneers, traders, or soldiers, meeting strangers along the way. Today, even if you are not adventurous, you live in the most mobile country in the world. You may be among 40 percent of people who move an average of 676 miles away from where they were raised, first for college and then later for jobs. Or, among the 20 percent of people contemplating a retirement relocation, often at a distance from other family members, friends, and familiar resources.

Every day you engage with more strangers and with greater diversity than any other generation in history experienced in an entire life. You live, work, play, and pray with people who are not like you. They have different backgrounds and were shaped by different experiences. They speak different languages, practice different religions, belong to different racial and ethnic groups, and have different ancestral histories. Some work in different time zones and are governed by different laws. You also encounter greater gender diversity as women take roles conventionally held by men. In fact, you probably know people who question the nature of gender itself, challenging traditional definitions and gender-based norms. Adding to the complexity, you connect face-to-face in real time and in virtual space, using technologies and social media platforms you might not fully understand and may not trust.

Survival Instincts Collide

All the while, you face another challenge you may not appreciate. Hardwired into your brain are two competing primitive survival instincts you inherited from your ancestors: the instinct to connect with others and the instinct to be cautious—or even fearful—of those who are not like you and your kin. A study by the Ontario Institute for Studies in Education shows that as early as six to nine months of age, we prefer the faces of people from our own race. Then, as we grow, we bond with people like us in many ways, including, according to a recent study published in *Psychological Science*, in simple daily rituals, preferring those people who share rituals with us over those who do not.

Your selective, protective instinct to be cautious can easily create challenges for you in your job, as you travel, and even in your neighborhood. It can be especially difficult when others' worldviews are unfamiliar or so nuanced that you can't appreciate their importance. It is easy these days to cross a boundary and unintentionally violate another person's deeply and dearly held beliefs. You can offend someone without knowing that you've done it. That is, until conflicts erupt.

Cultural, language, religious, life experience, ethnic, gender, and worldview diversity within ever-larger and more complicated groups of people create new demands on your time, energy, and attention. Can you manage it all? Might you be reaching your limit? British anthropologist and evolutionary psychologist Sir Robin Dunbar would say you are.

Dunbar's Number

I had been working to understand my network connections for several years before the 2010 publication of *How Many Friends Does One Person Need?* In his book, Sir Robin Dunbar placed the upper limit of connections one individual can manage well at 150 people. This has been known as "Dunbar's number" ever since. It explains the feeling people have when they begin the NetworkSage journey, especially during the first ACTSage step to become *aware* of all the people in their networks: overwhelm.

Dunbar's number is the maximum number of people with whom you can maintain consistent, face-to-face contact and for whom you can feel some emotional affinity. Dunbar suggests that this number has been our limit as humans for millennia. As evidence, he cites examples from historical records in English villages from the eleventh century and even farther back in history to Neolithic villages. He cites studies of tribal societies and military units dating back to the Roman era. He also references communities of Hutterites and the Amish in North America today, which split up when the group size reaches 150, having noticed that mutual obligation and reciprocity break down in a group larger than that.

There is other evidence of Dunbar's number in modern society as well. Those who send holiday greetings send an average of sixty-eight cards to households with about 150 people total. In academia, a study of twelve disciplines from the sciences and the humanities showed that scholars could follow the work of between 150 and 200 others. When an academic discipline becomes larger than that, it splits into subdisciplines. Businesses with fewer than 150 people work well on a person-to-person basis, but companies larger than that need a formal hierarchy. In companies with far more than 150 people, employees have more illnesses and absences.

The larger the group and the more complex your life circumstances, the more you need interpersonal and networking skills, and that takes brainpower. The 150-person limit suggested by Dunbar is set by the relationship between the size of the neocortex—the outer surface layer of the brain—and the size of a manageable group. Larger groups require more neocortical capacity to help keep track of changes and shifts that happen within groups. Why is that important? For your ancestors, alliances with others increased the chance of survival. For you, alliances help you to be happy, feel secure, raise children, achieve economic security, and enjoy life.

Dunbar's number of 150 might seem small in today's world, but managing even that number is demanding. Within a group that size, you expect to be known by the others. You would not need to introduce yourself or describe who you are, where you are from, or what you do for a living. You'd be offended if someone from the group met you on the street and didn't acknowledge you. Even if you could not recall their name, you would know where you stand in their world, and they would know where they stand in yours. You'd be more likely to loan each other money or possessions. You'd be more willing to share knowledge and connections to help one another find mates, housing, and jobs. You would know who could be trusted with a secret and who could not.

Connection Dynamics

Within Dunbar's number of 150 are groups of smaller sizes. The first is an innermost group of close connections of only three to five people you see at least weekly. The second is a slightly larger group of ten to fifteen people you see at least monthly. The death of one of these people would devastate you, which is why social psychologists call this your "sympathy group." The third is a larger group of thirty people you see several times a year. Recent studies of two contemporary groups of hunter-gatherers—in the Philippines and the Republic of the Congo—demonstrated how these smaller-size groups work in a fundamental, important way. In these cases, the three levels of social structure determined how food was shared. People shared the most food with those who were their closest social connections and then progressively less food with those in the two larger, more distant social spheres. Might you do likewise in similar ways today, sharing an essential commodity like your time or attention with your closest connections rather than those who are more distant?

Connectivity in smaller groups might sound simple, but it's not. It is more complicated because when people are closer to you, you have more intimate interactions with them, requiring even more care and attention. Stephen Covey articulated this well. For that reason, if you allow a new person into one of your smaller circles, it is likely that someone else will drop out. This happens throughout life as you leave home, marry, or form life-partner bonds and lose touch with friends to focus on your partner, your partner's friends, and especially your in-laws. It happens as you have children, change jobs, or relocate.

If you know even a little about the brain, these limits on group size make sense. As important as your brain is, it's relatively small, accounting for only about 2 percent of your total body weight. Despite its small size, it is an energy hog, using about 20 percent of your total energy. Some of that energy is spent helping you make sense of everything around you, including other people and your always-changing social world. Do that well and you build social capital. Just like money in the bank, it will be there when you need it. This is the reason there seems to be a limit to group size. You need to remember who is who, how various people relate to one another, and how they relate to you. All that information helps you accomplish what you want and get what you need from others, especially when you go to them for help. The brain expends a lot of energy handling all of that for you, and for good reason.

Your life and our society depend on your ability to introspect, reflect on your own feelings and beliefs, and attempt to understand the minds and beliefs of others to get what you want—all the while getting along with them. Experts call this tapestry of connection *theory of mind*. You were not able to do this as an infant, but eventually you learned. As a small child, you learned what would get you a cookie from the babysitter, for example. As a teen, you accomplished something even more complicated and learned how to win car keys from your dad. As an adult with a new baby, you learned that naming your child after the father's relatives creates closer kinship bonds (it does!) with in-laws.

As described by Dunbar, imagine the brain resources expended by Shakespeare to tell the story of *Othello*. Shakespeare *intends* that the audience *believe* that Iago *wants* Othello to *suppose* that Desdemona *loves* Cassio and he in turn *loves* her. What a feat of theory of mind! What an expenditure of brain resources for Shakespeare, the actors, and the audience!

Today's Connection Complications

Take that story, place it in the context of work life today, and imagine the added complexity. Make the stage a multigenerational, multiethnic, multiracial, multilingual, gender-fluid workplace large enough to cross time zones. Ask the actors on this stage to communicate in traditional ways and to also use asynchronous email, voicemail, and text messages. Allow firewalls to screen out some important messages as spam, adding to hurt feelings and causing relationship damage that needs to be repaired. Waiting in the wings, place Wall Street analysts, company shareholders, customers, and media reporters, each with different demands, cheaper prices, better performance, environmental sustainability, and corporate social responsibility. Fill the audience with critics and regulators from different governments setting different and sometimes contradictory rules. At work and outside of it, pressure the actors to respond instantly on a variety of communication and social media platforms. To this, add the reality of the actors' lives outside of work: the needs of family, friends, households, inevitable diseases, or long-distance caregiving. Toss in an occasional delayed flight, snowstorm, or school cancellation. Then imagine the need to build new connections when old ones are disrupted by divorce, job relocation, military deployment, retirement, or death.

Even if this description does not fit your life perfectly, it may come close. It may also help you understand the lives of those around you and see that, as compared with your ancestors—and even someone a generation ago—everyone today lives in a world more complicated than they could have imagined. Yes, your brain is working very hard to keep it all straight. No wonder there are limits. Does it therefore follow that all of us face the same limits?

Your Number

Others might feel social-connection limits, but what about you? Can you manage more people than Dunbar suggests?

Yes, some people can. I've seen them do it. It's not just about the size of your brain; other factors are involved as well. If you are healthy, energetic, and well organized, you can manage more. It helps if you have a smart device and the support of a great assistant, spouse, or life partner. It helps if you connect with people who have those assets and resources too. It helps if you and others are psychologically resilient, capable of reciprocity, and can forgive when slights occur. If everyone knows how to be mutually supportive, all the better.

Even under the best circumstances, however, there is a limit to the number of other people you can manage well. We all exhaust our bandwidth, hit a wall, and feel overwhelmed at some point. It is never a question of *if* but *when* and *how* that will happen.

It is common to feel that limit when a new stage of life places new demands on you. For example, finding a mate is one of the most energy-draining things your brain will ever do, and understandably so, since it's a high-risk decision. A poor choice can mean you don't reproduce or, if you do, that you and your offspring will not survive to keep our human race going. From an evolutionary perspective, those are very high stakes. The fate of humanity today does not rest on your decision, but when you choose a life partner, the quality of your personal health, happiness, and success are on the line. Select the right mate and your life can flourish. Select the wrong one and you can face abuse or poverty, especially if you are a woman and have children. If you're at the partner-seeking stage of life, you may have drifted away from some people or stopped making new connections to conserve the energy you need to manage the search.

You may hit your limit once you find a partner. As a married person, you connect with in-laws, your spouse's friends and colleagues, and maybe your spouse's former spouse and children from a prior marriage. Have a first child? Children come with lots of connections. Have a second child? You haven't added one more person to your family; you've added an exponentially large number of teachers, coaches, and parents of your child's friends. Buying a house increases the number of people you need to help keep it in good shape. Getting a promotion or retiring from the workforce changes your connections for sure!

You could reach your limit during times of personal, family, health, or workplace crises as well. You may manage many connections easily when you're healthy, employed, and rested. However, if you lose a job, your company merges with another, a tree crashes through your roof, or you're sitting up nights with a sick child, you may be unable to manage more than yourself and those helping you with the crisis at hand. If circumstances require you to care for another adult—a friend, spouse, or older relative—you are certain to hit a limit as you manage not only your needs and networks but many of their needs and networks too. Times like those can require you to cut back on other commitments and connections until life returns to normal.

You may also reach a limit if your lifestyle or life decisions create conflicts within important people in your life and require more of your energy to manage. One example comes from a NetworkSage couple who were the first in their families to graduate from college and have professional careers. The combination of their success and their decision to delay having children to pay off school loans and further their careers caused conflicts with family, some friends, and church clergy. The couple worked hard to maintain a détente within those important groups of people, draining them of the energy to form new friendships with others who could have been more supportive.

You may even reach your personal limit *before* Dunbar's number of 150 as well. Does your career require you to perform at your best for long periods of time? In that case, you may need to limit your connections to people who understand your need to pass up late evenings in favor of a good night's rest. Is your career in the armed services, as a first responder, or provider of emergency care? If so, your connections may be limited to those who understand your work can be traumatizing, and you may require support to recover from a deployment or particularly tough day on the job. Does your job require travel? If so, your friends may be limited to those who can accept you'll miss birthday parties and other events without making you feel guilty about it. Are you a senior and no longer able to drive safely at night? If so, you may need to limit friends to those who understand and cooperate in scheduling outings during daylight hours.

Social Media Number

Since there is a limit, what about social media networks? Will social media networks lead to a larger number of connections? Probably not. A study by Sir Robin Dunbar found that we limit the size of our online groups, just as we do off-line. Women averaged 166 Facebook friends, and men, just 145. Further, people said only 28 percent of Facebook friends were "genuine" or "close" friends, and on average, there were only four they would turn to in a crisis.

As relatively new in human history, only time will tell if social media will net positive or negative. Early studies indicate the impact is mixed. Some report positive results. Older people using Facebook, Skype, and instant messaging, for example, report less loneliness, fewer depressive symptoms, and decreased hypertension and diabetes, a clear benefit to them. Social media helps people form connections and learn from others who share common needs, especially when those needs arise from stigmatizing conditions. An example is new mothers with perinatal depression who are reluctant to reach out off-line but who can find support online. Social networks help people share their individual experiences and needs during disasters and, my personal favorite, to people watch as we once did in town squares. Social media provides support connections when friends die, as shown by Northwestern University computational social science expert William R. Hobbs. His study showed a 30 percent increase in interactions and continuing higher levels of interaction for two years among friends when one of the group dies. According to Dunbar, as an added benefit in today's highly mobile world, since friendships "degrade" and become acquaintances in the absence of regular contact, social media may slow the rate at which that happens.

Among reports of social media's negative impact, the more groups you join on Facebook, the greater your stress and possible risk, especially if your groups are diverse. That is because behavior acceptable to some connections, like friends, may be unacceptable to others, like family, employers, or customers. This is a factor to consider, given half of parents follow adult children and half of employers say they've not hired someone because of a Facebook post. Comparing yourself to others on Facebook is also more likely to lead to feelings of depression than comparing yourself to others off-line, as has been demonstrated in studies of thirty-five thousand participants across fourteen countries. Teens with more social media friends have higher levels of cortisol, a measure of stress.

Modern-day social media can scale indefinitely, but you can't. On social media, you can post, "like," "share," and "friend," engaging your real- and virtual-life connections there. In real life, you need more than that. You need the people in the eight networks we'll explore in part 2, but first, let's be certain you're in the driver's seat for the road ahead.

Key Points

- You are hardwired to connect with others.
- The quality of your connections determines your health, wealth, success, and happiness.
- Social complexity is far greater in today's world.
- There is a limit to how many connections you can maintain and manage well.
- You can engage with virtual-life connections on social media, but you need face-to-face connections as well.

Chapter 3
You Belong in the Driver's Seat

IMAGINE THAT, LIKE ME, you made a list of the people in all your networks. Then imagine that, from that list, you made a shorter list of those who are most important to you. Would your name be on that short list? If you are like me and others I know, it wouldn't. Yet it should be. And once it's there, it should remain there, except in rare circumstances and then only for brief times.

As one NetworkSage reminded me, that's easy to say and hard to do. "Every time there is a crisis," she told me, "I am the one who falls off my list. So many people say to 'put on your own oxygen mask first.' But life is not a flight emergency. Sometimes crises happen suddenly, but more often they build a little at a time and then can take weeks and months to resolve. If you're not taking care of yourself in the meantime, you're toast. You're not much good to anyone, including you!"

She was right. You need to claim your place on your own list. Self-sacrifice is often honored and sometimes is necessary, but it must be balanced with the recognition of the important place you hold as one who brings very special and unique value to the world. For that reason, not only must you be *on* the list; you must be at the *top*. This may seem like a bold statement, or even a self-centered and selfish one. My rationale, however, is anything but and comes from two observations. The first one is about your uniqueness. The second is about your role as the connector-in-chief across all your networks.

Appreciate Your Uniqueness

Your genes and fingerprints are only the beginning of your uniqueness. Consider, for a moment, your family network. You are a descendent of an estimated five hundred generations of ancestors who have lived since the dawn of civilization. These people provided you with far more than genes. They passed down what they learned as they lived, loved, suffered, and died from one generation to the next. Your understanding of human history, your imagination of what their lives were like, and older relatives' memories can help you appreciate the value of that legacy. Knowing that my mom did not live in a home with hot running water until she was in high school, for example, gave me an appreciation for the hardships my grandmother faced as a widow raising six children alone. It also explained the work ethic she passed on to future generations. Like me, you are here today not solely as the beneficiary of genetics but also as the culmination of life experiences like those passed down through five hundred generations. Each one of us is the pinnacle of our family lineage, equipped to leave a unique imprint on the world. How amazing is that!

What's more, you connect with people who enrich and support your life because of the culmination of their lineage histories. Not just their family lineages but other lineages as well. In your networks are people whose talents as educators, physicians, attorneys, business managers, architects, builders, clergy, and artists derive from skills developed by those who came before them in those fields. It is estimated that more than one hundred billion people have lived in human history. Their lives contribute to your life now. Thanks to them, you are healthy, educated, enriched, spiritually aware, and socially supported. Thanks to them, you have meaningful work, a comfortable home, and enabling technology. Thanks to them, you have access to vibrant art and music. Thanks to them, you can anticipate a longer, better life than they could have imagined.

Their creations provide you with greater assets than have been available at any other time in history. Never has anyone had such a rich combination of ancestral and modern resources as you have now. Understand your uniqueness, claim your rightful place, steward those resources well, and you will achieve your potential to succeed in whatever you do. That is the value of human capital and the result when you use it well.

Own Your Chief-Connector Role

Your connector-in-chief role is another reason I urge you to claim your place. As you explore your networks, you will find that some people are in more than one of them. It's common for a friend to be a colleague, or for a fitness buddy to be a neighbor and attend the same church, for example. Many small-business owners rely on their spouse to help with IT and be a sounding board for ideas or management challenges. Regardless of the number of people who appear in more than one network, however, there is only one person who appears in all your networks: you. You are the single common member and the common connector across them all.

This connector-in-chief role means that, though each of your networks may appear to be its own silo separate from the others, it is not. We try to compartmentalize life into "work" and "life" spheres or into "social" or "career" areas, but in truth, our networks never function separately. Much as we might like and as often as some experts recommend, compartmentalizing is impossible.

Whatever impacts you in any one network can impact those in other networks because you connect them all. Receive good news from your child's *education network*—college admission with a full scholarship— and the smile on your face will make you attractive to others and might help you land new business. It might ease tensions in your *family network* caused by financial worries about tuition bills and may boost your *social network* standing among friends. On the other hand, if your child's *health network* delivers bad news, it can impact each of your networks for weeks or months to come. Lose your job, your marriage, or your money, and that can shatter your belief in divine protection and connections with your *spiritual network* or end your willingness to be a generous volunteer in your *social and community network*. The death of a loved one will ripple through all your networks, possibly for years to come. No network is ever isolated from the others because you, the connector-in-chief, link them all together.

Because of your uniqueness and connector-in-chief role, it is not selfish to place yourself at the top of your list. In fact, I believe you have the *right* to claim that place. When you do, your successes will honor the hopes and justify the sacrifices of those who came before you. What's more, I believe you have the *responsibility* to claim your place. When you do, your successes will create not only a better life for you but also a better world for others, blessing those who come after you.

Distinguish Connection Types

The number of connections we have as children is quite large, and as adults, that number grows larger still. Organizing them into networks and groups within networks will help you to remember and manage them better.

There is another key consideration as well, based on the type of connection you have with them. In this case, I am not referring to whether they are a life partner, child, parent, colleague, boss, physician, hairdresser, or friend. Those distinctions are important but often aren't a sufficient framework for decision-making about whether or how you connect or spend your energy. That is especially true when you are overloaded and face conflicting commitments.

Understanding these connection types might be easier if I tell you how I first knew this could be important. The story begins one evening in London. A client meeting ended earlier that day, and Europeans could leave for home. The other American attendee and I, however, could not depart until the next morning's flights to the United States.

We decided to enjoy London theater but were interested in different shows. Going our separate ways, we agreed to meet at the hotel afterward, enjoy a nightcap, and trade reviews of the performances. That's important to know because of what happened next.

In the taxi returning to the hotel that night, her driver learned she was a visitor leaving the next day. He offered to take her to Heathrow Airport; she agreed to his proposed pickup time. Though she was an experienced international traveler, this was her first trip to London. My work took me to London often those days, so I knew there was extra security for US-bound flights. The taxi driver had not allowed for the extra time she would need. I cautioned her that she would face multiple screenings, suggesting that if he did not arrive at least fifteen minutes early, she get another taxi to make her flight on time. "But I promised him," she argued.

Because we were on different flights returning to different cities, I don't know if she took my advice. At best, she was stressed making her flight. Worse, she might have missed it altogether. I do know that back in the States she had a husband. They had several young children, and she'd already been away for three days. Given the need, I could imagine she'd give her life for them. Yet, in this situation, she argued for keeping a promise to a man she met once and would never see again, over the promises she'd made to a man she pledged love and to the children she'd given life.

The story haunted me for years as I wondered why. I saw others make similar choices and caught myself doing it. People who hear this story say my client was demonstrating her integrity by keeping her word. That may be true. What can we do when promises collide? Is there a good way to help you resolve the dilemma? I think there is. That way is to make distinctions between the types of connections you have with others. In NetworkSage terms, these types are *primary*, *support*, and *transactional*. When you've learned about how I define these connections, you might create your own refinements. Knowing about mine will give you a head start.

Primary Connections

People are primary connections when they are closest to your heart and uppermost in your mind. You love them, think about them each day, and celebrate when wonderful things happen for them. You worry when they're ill and would be devastated if they severed ties with you or passed away. If you are responsible for all or part of their lives, you are willing to make the extra effort when they need you. Conversely, if they are responsible for all or part of your life, you trust them to provide what you need.

Experts like Sir Robin Dunbar, who I've already mentioned, say this is a very small group and is probably limited to the three to five people who are your innermost circle of friends and family, along with a slightly larger group of ten to fifteen people that social psychologists refer to as your sympathy group. In your personal life, this would include your children, your spouse or life partner, your parents, your very best friends, and perhaps even a pet. In your work life, this would include your boss, your biggest clients, or your direct reports. Although experts would not place you on that list, I do. My rationale is based on your uniqueness and network centrality as I've already described. It will become even clearer why you should be on that short list of primary connections when I describe the role of those who are support and transactional connections.

When you have a primary connection with someone in your life— yourself, a spouse, children, best friend, boss, or important client—you have intentions for them. To realize those intentions, in most cases you need the help from others. Those people are your support connections.

Support Connections

People are support connections when they help achieve the intentions, goals, and dreams you have for those who are your primary connections. This is a larger group of people. For example, if you are a parent, your children are primary connections, and to realize your intentions for them, you engage others: babysitters, teachers, doctors, coaches, clergy, and the parents of your children's friends. These people are the support connections that help you assure your children are safe, healthy, well educated, enculturated into your traditions, and, eventually, launched successfully into adult life.

In your marriage, to help a spouse trying to quit smoking, you might suggest other couples join you as support connections for fun outings that will not trigger an urge for a cigarette rather than those outings that do. In your social life, to help a best friend with a chronic condition, you might engage other friends as support connections to encourage a healthy lifestyle, like good food choices when you dine together. In your career, to help your boss succeed, you engage your own staff, vendors, and consultants as support connections to help.

On your own behalf, you have support connections with physicians to help you be healthy, therapists to help you resolve personal dilemmas, and friends to help you have fun. You engage the support of coaches to improve your career performance, and spiritual guides to deepen your spiritual life. If you own a home, you have support connections with electricians and plumbers who help care for it. You may also have accountants who assure your taxes are done correctly and attorneys who develop legal documents to protect loved ones.

Although you relate to these people when you are with them, you are not in a relationship with them in the same way as you are with those who are primary connections. You would be sad if your child's teacher passed away, and it would be disruptive if your physician or business coach retired and you needed to find a new one. It would be unfortunate if friends declined to help you support a loved one trying to quit smoking, lose weight, or manage a chronic disease. You would miss a favorite clergyperson who relocated to another state, and it would be time-consuming if your accountant closed her practice and you needed to find another. Those situations are far less impactful than losing someone who is a primary connection, however. Support connections can be replaced far more easily.

Everyone else you engage with during the day, including some you may include on your network lists, are transactional connections.

Transactional Connections

People are transactional connections when you engage with them for a limited time and for a limited purpose, as you do with taxi drivers, airline flight crew, post office clerks, bank tellers, and wait staff at restaurants. This is the largest of the three groups. Some encounters are random, isolated, and only happen once. Some happen regularly if you frequent the same restaurants, bars, banks, and coffee shops and get to know the people there, and especially if they provide excellent customer service and make it a point to know you.

Transactional connections provide you with goods and services that ease the many daily tasks in your routine. You relate to them during your encounters, but you are not in a relationship with them as you are with your primary connections, and they are far more replaceable than those who are support connections. Though they are the most easily replaced, that does not mean they are unimportant. Even transactional connections can be transformative, as you will see later in two wonderful stories, one about a blueberry and another about how a stranger's smile saved a man's life.

Transactions can also be memorable, some for positive reasons and others for negative ones. The bank teller who recognized that my signature on a corporate check was counterfeit comes to mind. Her quick reaction not only saved me headaches but helped the bank locate and eventually prosecute a counterfeiting ring targeting small businesses. Or, consider the opposite: the teller at my mom's bank who recently allowed me into her safe deposit box without checking my ID or signature. This security dry run was my mom's idea, and it was a good one: imagine the consequences had I been a stranger intent on stealing its contents. If my client missed her flight home from London, the taxi driver wasn't someone she'd soon forget.

Distinction, Not Discrimination

Making a distinction like this among your connections is not discrimination. The mutual support, courtesy, and cooperation we have with one another—even with transactional connections—creates the social glue that underpins all human advancement. Getting along and treating others well is something most of us aim to achieve. In fact, some people, like prospective employers dining with job candidates, watch interactions with transactional connections to assess the candidate's character. Some people dining with prospective mates do as well. Rather, these distinctions provide a framework for setting boundaries to help you decide whether and where to spend your energy. That is important because you probably manage large numbers of connections and find that commitments collide regularly.

In failing to make distinctions, you risk diverting energy from higher-priority to lower-priority connections. In my own life, only in retrospect do I understand the problems caused by not making these distinctions. Before exploring pit crews and networks and without this terminology to help, I didn't set good boundaries. I allowed support and transactional connections to deprive me of the time, energy, and patience I needed and wanted for primary connections. Too often, those I engaged (and was paying) as a support connection turned the tables and made me support them. Accountants and attorneys who missed deadlines and doctors and hairdressers who required appointments but then kept me waiting are examples.

I think that's what happened to my client in London. I know her to be a person of integrity and a caring wife and mother. When she resisted my advice to depart the hotel for the airport earlier than the taxi driver's proposed time, I believe she lacked a way to decide between conflicting commitments: one commitment to a transactional connection and other commitments to primary connections. Thus, she held them equally important and placed the most important ones— herself and her family—at risk.

Making Distinctions

Only you can make these distinctions, and unfortunately, there are no hard-and-fast rules to apply as you do. There are, however, some tips that may help. First, the distinctions you make may be different from those of family, friends, or colleagues. Someone who is a support connection for you might be a transactional connection for others. Here is an example: although there is no cancer in my family, I get regular mammograms and other routine cancer screenings. I have no reason to fear the results and feel no loyalty to the medical center where I go for them. I will visit a different one next time if the parking or the hours are more convenient. After all, though it is an important connection, for me it's just transactional. In contrast, my friends who have survived breast cancer get mammograms at the same medical center each time. The films are taken by the same technician, they are interpreted by the same radiologist, and they know the results immediately. For my friends, the medical center and its staff are support connections. If their cancer reoccurs, those at the medical center might become primary connections.

Second, the type of connections you have with someone can change over time. A primary connection today may become a support connection in the future. Your physician today, for example, is a support connection. If you relocate to a new town, your connection ends once your medical records are transferred. Your boss is a primary connection today but tomorrow may be a support connection if you leave your job but remain in a mentoring relationship. A colleague may be a support connection today but become a primary connection if you fall in love and marry. In the case of one happily married couple I know, their current primary connection began as a transactional one when he bought a shirt from her at a specialty menswear clothing store here in Philadelphia.

Defining these three types of connections tells the story about my client in London in a new way. At the time, four of my client's primary connections were involved: herself, her husband, and her two children.

I was the support connection, using the benefit of my experience to help her meet one of her goals: getting home to loved ones. The taxi driver was a transactional connection, and he may have had even greater negative impact than I've already mentioned. You see, her husband had a long local commute to work, and her mother, also a primary connection, had come to help care for their children while my client was away. She was set to fly home as my client's own flight was landing. If my client missed her flight, there were disruptive consequences for important primary connections. At best, she was stressed when she made the flight. At worst, if she missed the flight, her husband and children would spend another day without her, and her husband would be left without her mother's help on a workday.

You will find each of these connection types as you explore your networks, beginning with the next chapter.

Key Points

- Claim your rightful place at the center of your networked life.
- Appreciate your uniqueness and connector-in-chief role.
- Distinguish among the primary, support, and transactional connections you have with others.
- Making distinctions is not discrimination but a way to decide whether and where to spend time and energy and how to decide between competing commitments.

part 2
exploring network territory

KEY TO REALIZING THE superpower in your networks is knowing where to look to find it, which is how a *network information architecture* helps. The need for an organizing method like this one was clear from my own initial experience. Even after weeks of list making, without a reminder of where to look for connections, I forgot important people. This happened to others who joined me on this journey. To help them— and now you—recall people more accurately, I experimented with various ways to organize connections into networks, testing to assure they made sense.

The one you will read about in this part of the book is intuitive and easy to remember. It arranges connections into eight networks that support your life as an adult. It is more comprehensive than frameworks companies use to manage employee human resources and customer relations because it includes aspects of life outside the workplace. It is more expansive than career or social networks you build through LinkedIn or Facebook because it includes connections not normally made there. It is more complete than what financial planners, estate planners, or attorneys use when they advise you. It helps you find all your network connections wherever they may be, in each part of your life. It also helps you identify important connections that might be missing. As a bonus, it makes the process much faster and more accurate than it was for me when I began.

Five Birthright Networks

I call the first five of the eight networks *birthright networks* because you were born into them. Your parents created them to meet your basic needs for family ties, physical care, educational opportunity, spiritual support, and social interaction. You could not have thrived without them and, in fact, would not have survived. This was obvious when you were an infant, but it remains true throughout your life.

- *Family Network.* This network includes your family of origin and other families that you have been a part of, including the one you created for your children and any former families from past relationships.
- *Health and Vitality Network.* This network includes those who help you to be healthy and fit. It also includes those who help you look good since appearance is important.
- *Education and Enrichment Network.* This network includes those involved in your formal years of education and as you prepare for a job. It also includes those who provide enrichment experiences outside of formal educational settings.
- *Spiritual Network.* This network includes those in congregations and houses of worship and connections with others outside of those formal settings with whom you develop your sense of what is spiritual and meaningful in life.
- *Social and Community Network.* This network includes your neighbors and friends as well as those in your community, clubs, or civic organizations, and your virtual connections through social media.

Three Coming-of-Age Networks

As you enter adulthood, you progress through milestones considered to be markers of maturity: leaving home, finishing school, becoming financially independent, finding a mate, and having a child. As you do, you mature into three additional networks I call *coming-of-age networks*. Coming-of-age networks do not replace your birthright networks; they build upon them.

- *Career Network.* This network includes people in your workplace: your boss, direct reports, colleagues, and cross-functional or support teams. It also includes clients and customers outside your workplace and others in your chosen field. Even at retirement, this network supports you with retiree benefits and enduring connections created during your years in the workforce.
- *Home and Personal Affairs Network.* This network includes those who help you protect, maintain, and improve your household and personal property and who support your need for legal and financial advice.
- *Ghost Network.* This network includes people who are not currently physically present in your life because they have passed away, moved away, or drifted away as your life changed. You've been gathering ghosts from the beginning of your life, but as you come of age, you gain greater awareness of who they are and how they have shaped you.

In ideal circumstances, the connections in your birthright networks—the first five—were wiser, smarter, more experienced and better resourced than you. They helped you learn, celebrated your successes, and delighted in your developmental milestones. They comforted you during stressful times and made harsh realities more tolerable. These birthright networks change as you grow up, but you never outgrow the need for what they provide. In ideal circumstances, the connections in your coming-of-age networks—the remaining three—help you find jobs, mates, homes, and advisers. They support you and help when you ask. They are wise mentors, give you good advice, and provide you with quality goods and services. They help you build a better life for yourself and for those people, causes, and ventures you care about.

If your early life was not ideal, however, your birthright networks may have failed to give you the support they were built to provide. Worse, they may have abused you, made learning difficult, downplayed your achievements, and harmed your physical and mental health. They may have limited your educational opportunities and isolated you from the social support you needed during stressful times, leaving you to cope alone. If your coming-of-age networks are not ideal, they can make your job difficult, sabotage your career, and harm your reputation. They can damage your finances, make homeownership a costly mistake, and leave you unprepared for retirement. If your circumstances were not—or are not—ideal, there are probably holes to fill, not just in your heart but also in your networks. Understanding networks will help you decide which resources can help you recover and get back on track. It may also help you see how amazingly strong and resilient you are to have reached this point in your life despite the obstacles in your way.

Chapter 4
Family Networks

A Young NetworkSage

KRISSIE IS EVIDENCE THAT even a young child can become a NetworkSage. Like many modern families, seven-year-old Krissie's is not simple to describe. Both sets of grandparents had divorced and remarried, creating four blended, extended families for her. She had eight grandparents and six great-grandparents.

When her maternal grandmother, Ellen, remarried, her new husband, Mike, had grown children of his own and a grandchild on the way. At busy family gatherings, no one noticed that the usually outgoing Krissie was very shy around Mike's family, rarely approaching them on her own even though one of his daughters was about to get married and Krissie was going to be in the wedding.

Then Grandma Ellen noticed a change. One day, Krissie walked directly up to Mike's daughter with confidence and declared, "Grandpa Mike is your father, so that means you are my aunt. When the wedding day comes, your new husband will be my uncle." Then she turned to Mike's son and said, "Grandpa Mike is your father. That means you are my uncle and your wife is my aunt. When your baby comes, she will be my cousin."

What happened? Grandma Ellen, a NetworkSage herself, invited Krissie to learn about her own networks one day. They talked about the people in Krissie's life and drew pictures of the networks Krissie named: her immediate family, her teachers, her doctor and dentist. When it came to her friends, she listed them grouped by the things they liked to do together: yoga, art class, and T-ball. This gave Ellen the chance to explain Krissie's extended families, and for the first time, Krissie learned how everyone was related.

Ellen believes the drawings helped Krissie understand her complicated family network, giving her the confidence to approach her new aunts and uncles. Krissie didn't stop there, though. A few months later, at an even larger extended family gathering with Ellen's relatives, Krissie continued her family network explorations with everyone, going to each person to sort out how she was related. At seven years old, Krissie became the youngest NetworkSage.

Understanding how she was related was the first step for Krissie in creating connections with everyone. It was a step worth taking, not just for today but for her future. The people in her family network are top professionals in a variety of fields and are deeply caring, engaged people with large networks of their own. In a few short years as she comes of age, Krissie will have advice, information, and their connections to support her. The trusting connections she is building now will increase the likelihood she will reach out when the time comes and take advantage of what they will generously offer.

Network Role and Value

Given the importance of your family network, it's a good place to begin your exploration. This network made the most important contributions to your life. Most obvious is the contribution to your genetics. The longevity and disease conditions of your ancestors are now part of your medical history and shape the advice you get today. Your physicians take that into account in rating your disease risks and urging you to practice a healthy lifestyle to reduce them. Life insurance underwriters use that information to determine whether to insure you and what premiums to charge. Your attorney and financial planner consider it in developing last wills, powers of attorney, retirement plans, and advance directives.

Your family network gave you far more than genes, however. It created all your other birthright networks, determining your early experiences of families, health care, education, sports, spirituality, and neighborhood life. It set expectations for your level of achievement and helped you along the way to succeed. If your extended family network supported your parents well, that lightened the workload and stress associated with childrearing. That helped make your parents and your home life happier and your life better overall.

It was the role of those in your family network to assure that you were supported, fed, and kept warm and safe from harm. They also tended to your social needs by cuddling, rocking, and holding you, which experts now know plays an important role in cognitive and emotional development. They intervened for you to assure your experiences in other birthright networks were positive, and if they succeeded in creating supportive networks, you grew up feeling accepted and loved wherever you went.

Along the way, your family network taught life lessons that might seem obvious but that are powerful because of how unconsciously you learned them. Among the many powerful lessons is the one about how families are organized and how multiple generations interact and support one another to seize opportunities and meet challenges. If your family today is organized or relates differently from your family of origin, you may have no helpful model to guide your way and might be struggling to do it well.

When Krissie's grandma Ellen grew up, for example, divorce was rare, and a nuclear family of two parents and children was the norm. Not so today. According to the US Census Bureau, as of 2016, fewer than 20 percent of American households are once-married couples with children. Single-parent families, headed by people who are divorced, widowed, or never married, and blended families like Krissie's are the most common family types. If you have a blended family now, your experience may be new for you, but it is also now the norm. Today, 65 percent of remarriages involve children from the prior marriage, and one of every three Americans is a stepparent, stepchild, stepsibling, or some other member of a blended family. Half of all Americans (and two-thirds of all women) have been, are now, or will eventually be in a step-kinship family relationship.

The trend toward increasing numbers of single-parent families is likely to continue. More adults today are single than married, fewer women in their thirties are married than ever in history, marriage rates are at an all-time low, and 55 percent of singles are not looking to get married at all. Many will have children nonetheless, and some may create new lifestyle models to make that easier. A small but growing trend, for example, are connections among several single women who share childcare and expenses. In the nineteenth century, an arrangement of this type was known as "Boston marriage."

These are not the only ways families have changed, however. Even "official" definitions of a family have changed to include a same-sex couple raising a child, an unmarried couple living together with a child, grandparents raising grandchildren, and married couples without children.

The definition of a parent has changed too. Medical technology now allows eggs and sperm to be provided by one person to another for the purposes of conceiving a child, and women become surrogate mothers by bearing children for others. A child born today could have several mothers by the time they enter preschool: one who donated an egg, a second who carried the fertilized egg to term, a third who adopted the baby at birth, and a fourth if the child's parents divorces and the father remarries. That same child could have more than one father as well.

All these changes are disruptive events but are by no means the only challenges families face. Today's career- and retirement-mobile society makes it likely that your family of origin and others you consider family live in distant towns, regions, and even countries. Only rarely can everyone in the family gather. Some may not be able to travel to be with you, even for an important event like your wedding. As a young parent, you may lack extended-family support for childrearing and need to find alternatives. As an adult child, you may need to travel a great distance to see your parents or help them when the need arises.

Even families that are otherwise intact can face disruptions and separation when a parent is an active duty or reserve military service member, has long workday commutes, travels extensively for work, or is incarcerated. These are increasingly common stressful events families face, as are financial and relationship problems, difficult pregnancies, premature births, job loss, and deaths of close family members. Stresses like these can create health, education, and achievement problems for everyone, behavior problems in children years later, and increased risk that children will be bullied at school.

Also as an adult are those who face one of the biggest family disruptions of all: aging alone without *any* family support. Called "elder orphans," some never married or had children. Most, however, did marry, cared for husbands and other family members, and are now the family's sole survivor. There are currently fourteen million elder orphans, a group destined to grow larger, not just because of the size of the baby boomer cohort but because one-third of boomers never had children at all.

Stable or disrupted, your family—and the other birthright networks they created for you—shaped your worldview. Long before you could understand alternatives and question whether their worldview was correct or in your best interests, it had a powerful influence on your future. I took diversity for granted, for example, until I got to college and got to know my roommate. That's because my family was a blended combination of different nationalities, immigrants and first-generation Americans, languages, cuisines, and religions, and our friends and my classmates were multiracial. She, on the other hand, had never met a person of another culture, race, or religion until she arrived on our Big Ten campus. Our first year on campus didn't come easy for her as she worked to adapt to a diverse student body. I, on the other hand, could direct my energy elsewhere.

Inside Family Networks

I organize this network into four different groups: a family of origin, your family today, a former family, and a "just like" family.

In these families are people who may be related to you in a variety of ways. For example, you may be related by blood, sharing a common ancestor. You may also be related by marriage or another legal action like a civil union or domestic partnership because of a choice you or your parents made. You may also be related by other legal actions that made you part of a family as a child or young person, for example, if you were in foster care, were adopted, were a ward, were a person in need of supervision, or were assigned a guardian by a court.

Families consist of people in a variety of roles: parents, surrogate parents, stepparents, adoptive parents, foster parents, siblings, half siblings, stepsiblings, adoptive siblings, foster siblings, and wards. Other family members include grandparents and, for most people, aunts, uncles, cousins, and in-laws. Some people consider nannies or exchange students who live with them to be family, and if you are like many Americans, you consider your beloved pet to be a member of your family as well.

1. Family of Origin

This is the family you were born into as a child. Your parents created this one for you. If you are a parent, this is the family you created for your children.

2. Your Family Today

As you matured, one milestone along the way to becoming an adult involved leaving your family of origin and creating your own family. In the past, this meant finding a spouse and having children. Today, you may be one of those creating new types of families as an unmarried person with a life partner, in a civil union, or as a single person raising children on your own. You might consider the person who donated an egg or sperm, or a surrogate who carried your child to term to be part of your family. You might be a widow or widower raising—or living with—children since the death of your spouse. You might also be a grandparent raising a grandchild. You might be a single person living with other singles in a family-style household, particularly if you are young or old, to share expenses and lighten the workload.

3. Former Family

If you—or your spouse or life partner—are divorced or separated, you and they have connections with people who were formerly family. Even if you had no children, you may have forged strong bonds with your former in-laws and might remain connected to them. Divorce or separation can stress those bonds and even break them but not necessarily. Especially if you had children or pets, you may have ongoing contacts with those who were once part of your family life.

4. "Just Like" Family

There may be people in your life unrelated by blood or marriage but whom you treat as family nonetheless. You might call them aunt or uncle to honor them as someone you hold dear. If you do have just-like family in your life, you include them in gatherings and important celebrations as if you are related. In today's highly mobile society, as young people relocate to pursue careers and older people relocate in retirement, creating loving and supportive bonds with others who serve traditional family roles can be nurturing and mutually supportive for everyone involved, as I've learned from my own experience as an adopted grandma.

Exploring Your Network

Beginning with your family of origin and thinking back to the time you were a child is a good way to explore family networks. Consider, for example, the kind of family your parents created for you, including brothers, sisters, and pets. Recall any friends or neighbors who, to you, felt just like family.

Recall celebrations and those who joined you for important milestone events, especially if they came from far away and you did not see them often. Recall disruptive circumstances, like separation, divorce, incarceration of your parents, or the death of a family member that changed the connections within your family and brought new people into your life.

Especially if you had grandparents or great-grandparents, they may have created a large extended family for you. You may know family stories that provide you with insights.

Consider how divorce, remarriage, or foster care changed connections with parents and siblings and how those connections have changed over time.

Recall the traditions your family created. Note whether you observe them now or pass them on to your children. This might include how you celebrate holidays, how you share workload, and whether you help others in need.

Key Points

- This network provides you with the care you need as a child and creates all five birthright networks.
- Your connections in these networks change as you mature, but you never outgrow the need for what they provide.
- Today's definition of a family has changed and is far more varied than in the past.

- Today's families are smaller, separated by career and retirement mobility, and disrupted, with once-married couples with children no longer the norm.
- A large—and growing—group of seniors have no family support at all.

Chapter 5

Health and Vitality Networks

Dr. Mom

I SUBSCRIBE TO AN email service that summarizes important health research. One reported on a study that said women, more than men, fail to fill their prescriptions. When they do fill their prescriptions, they fail to take the medicines as prescribed. Puzzled and curious to learn more, I called a friend who is an expert in that field. She confirmed what the research reported. In fact, she said it even applied to her. "I manage medications for me, my two boys, our dog, and my husband's grandfather." In the process, she paid less attention to her own health. She wasn't taking her own medicines as prescribed.

Like lots of people who work in health care—and many who don't—she was Dr. Mom. She was also Dr. Wife, Dr. Sister, Dr. Friend, Dr. Daughter, Dr. Daughter-in-Law, and Dr. Granddaughter, helping lots of people through the health care maze. She did that in addition to her job, managing the household, and fundraising for the local YMCA.

"Health care has a long way to go," she admitted. "Working women like me feel an extra burden because a doctor's work hours, my work hours, and the kids' school hours overlap. And when it comes to insurance company rules, don't get me started. I used vacation time to get a pap smear recently. When I got to the doctor's office, I learned that I'd booked the appointment two weeks before the date of last year's test, so it would not be covered. By the time the 'right' date came around two weeks later, I'd have to take off work again and the boys would be in basketball tournaments. I did a quick calculation and figured I'd be better off paying for it myself out of pocket than missing another half day of billable work. Can't the system be more flexible and convenient?"

Network Role and Value

If your health and vitality network functions well, it will do more than be flexible and convenient. It is the role of the people in this network to help you to enjoy longer life and better health. If they do, the value of this network extends beyond your health and drives straight to the heart of the value of human capital.

Public health experts have long known that wealth improves health. More recent studies show that the converse is also true: health improves wealth. With good support from this network, your personal productivity and earnings will be greater and you will have more energy for family, friends, and the communities you care about. If your children are healthy, they will be more prepared for school, miss fewer days of class, and learn more when they are there. They will attend school for more years, with each year associated with a 15 percent higher starting salary and a doubling in the rate of future salary increases.

If you have elderly parents and manage care for them or others, your loved ones will be healthier, reducing the chances you will need to leave the workforce or cut back on your work hours or other necessities to care for them. As a senior, you will be able to live independently, age well in place in your community, and avoid expensive hospitalizations and institutional care. If you are a business owner or manager, the good health of employees and their families will result in fewer days lost to illness, fewer disruptions from family caregiving, and lower health care costs for employees and dependents.

Good health benefits you directly and indirectly. Experts like Drs. David M. Mirvis and David Bloom estimate that over half the rate of economic growth in the United States over the past hundred years is the result of better health, and though both the wealthy and poor benefit, the poor benefit most. These benefits are important for us as a nation. Countries that are healthy are more likely to attract global talent and investment capital, which in turn provide you and your loved ones with enhanced opportunities for a better, more economically secure life.

Looking Good

If this network serves you well, you will also look better. That is important because your appearance is not a trivial concern. Although your health and some physical features determine whether others perceive you as attractive, personal grooming and attire go a long way toward helping you look good.

That matters for several reasons. Looking good helps boost your mood and self-esteem. It improves your standing with others since people make near-instant, unconscious judgments about you based on your appearance. If you doubt that, watch the initial reactions to Susan Boyle on *Britain's Got Talent*. Then notice the transformation as she sings. Neither the audience nor the judges believed such a beautiful voice could come from someone who did not look the part.

Attractive people wear a kind of halo. They are considered more able, trustworthy, cooperative, talented, kind, honest, and intelligent. Even a photo can lead people to judge whether a stranger is extroverted, agreeable, emotionally stable, and contentious, views that don't change when they meet and interact months later. Attractive people sell more products, attractive college professors get better student ratings, and attractive college students get better grades. Good grooming helps job candidates, even when interviewers claim they are not biased by how the candidate looks. For these reasons, good-looking people, on average, earn $230,000 more than unattractive people over the course of a lifetime. Oh, and attractive people are also more likely to marry.

Engaging This Network

If you find it difficult to get support from the medical part of this network, you are not alone. It is far more costly and complex than in times past. It can be difficult to get an appointment, and even when you do, the appointment time might be inconvenient and require you to miss work, your children to miss school, or you to wait long hours at a clinic. If you don't have a personal physician and seek care in an emergency department, you'll face even longer waits and higher costs.

If your health takes a turn for the worse and you are diagnosed with a chronic condition, you're likely to be diagnosed with another one every three years. Eventually, those chronic conditions can require multiple medications and radical changes in your lifestyle that can impact every one of your networks. Your care won't be coordinated by the health care system, at least not anytime soon, so you'll need to manage multiple specialists regardless of the burdens on your time or your ability to do so. If you are diagnosed with a life-threatening condition, the care you receive will be far more complicated and urgent, and the number of specialists whose support you need may be even greater. The emotional stress may outstrip anything you have ever experienced, and financial bankruptcy is a real possibility. Living in a rural area makes getting care even more difficult and, because of the travel involved, can be even more costly.

Today, internet resources can provide you with information and help you learn about your health and how to manage your conditions. The internet and social media can also connect you with others who can offer practical suggestions on how to manage as well. That said, there is no substitute for the experts you need in your health and vitality networks. At the very minimum, you should have access to primary medical and dental care. Pediatricians call this a "medical home," and that's a good way to think about it. Care in a medical home ensures that your medical records are complete. It improves your chances of preventing diseases before they occur and getting treatment for diseases if they do, so that you do not suffer complications. It also improves your chances of getting good referrals to specialists when you need them.

There is also no substitute for those people who help you to be fit, including family and friends who join you in active living and support healthy lifestyle choices and those trainers and teachers at fitness centers or yoga studios. If you are an older person, even someone to help assure your shoes fit correctly can be included here, as research shows that seniors with ill-fitting shoes have a lower quality of life. They have more pain, more difficulty getting healthy food, poorer general health, lower rates of physical activity, and less social engagement. They have limited mobility and more infections, anxiety, apathy, and falls, which harm well-being and independence.

Finally, you may one day need care support to help you cope during times of serious illness, after accidents, when you've had surgery, or if you become frail as you age. People who provide care support, such as managing complicated health needs, helping with daily-living activities and end-of-life care, help not only you but family and friends as well. They intervene with health care providers and other social support agencies and can coach family members and friends through stressful times to help reduce any stress or conflicts that arise.

Inside Health and Vitality Networks

I organize this network into nine different groups that are structured based on whether they provide you with basic or specialist care, whether you receive care in the community, in an institution, or in your home with the assistance of others, and whether they help you be fit and look good. I also include those who help you by providing care for your pets.

1. Primary and Specialist Health, Dental, and Vision Care

These people provide you with primary, specialty, and subspecialty care. They are the physicians in primary care, such as family medicine and internal medicine; for children, pediatrics; and for women, obstetrics and gynecology. Included in this network are the nurses, nurse practitioners, and physician assistants who see patients and support physicians in clinics.

Included as well are those who provide primary dental care, such as dentists and dental hygienists—individuals who are now recognized for the important role they play in the quality of your health, not just in the quality of your smile.

Optometrists, ophthalmologists, and opticians who provide primary and specialty vision care and correction are likewise on this list. Pharmacists and nutritionists are in this group since virtually everyone uses prescription or over-the-counter medicines, and nutrition is a way to get—and stay—healthy.

This group includes specialist physicians as well, like allergists, gastroenterologists, rheumatologists, oncologists, cardiologists, neurologists, dermatologists, and surgeons. Certain conditions require subspecialists, and those individuals are included in this network. Children may need the care of a pediatric gastroenterologist, for example, or seniors may need the care of a geriatric psychiatrist.

2. Primary and Specialist Mental Health Care

These people provide you with primary and specialty mental health care, including social workers, psychologists, psychiatrists, and psychoanalysts. Specialists in this field include those who work with certain techniques like hypnotherapy as well as those who specialize in certain conditions like smoking cessation, addiction, post-traumatic stress, weight loss, or learning disabilities.

3. Traditional and Alternative Health Care

These people offer you traditional and alternative health care and may include those who are the native healers of your family lineage or ethnicity. They are herbalists, shamans, medicine men and women, spirit healers, and faith healers. They help prevent diseases and treat physical and mental health problems. Included in this group are other alternative health practitioners, such as acupuncturists, massage therapists, chiropractors, and healing touch and Reiki practitioners.

1. Institution-Based Health Care

These people provide you with care in hospitals, rehabilitation centers, nursing homes, assisted-living centers, or hospices. Physicians, nurses, physical therapists, caseworkers, dieticians, pain-management and palliative-care experts, and pastoral care staff are all included in this group. Also included are those who provide the support services that keep the institution running well like administrators, building engineers, housekeepers, maintenance workers, and food service staff.

2. Fitness and Well-Being

These people help you maintain or improve your fitness and general sense of physical and mental well-being. Pilates teachers, yoga instructors, and trainers at your gym are examples. If you play a sport, your coaches, team members, or partners are part of this group. If fans are an important part of your sport, they are included here as well. If you join a regular morning walking group or weekend biking group, those people are in your health and vitality network.

3. Appearance

These people help you maintain and improve your appearance. Your hairdresser or barber, colorist, manicurist, tailor, and dry cleaner are examples, as are image consultants and personal shoppers.

4. Care Support

This group includes several types of connections. Often, all the people in this group are called caregivers. There are different types of caregivers, however, and it can be important to make those distinctions. Some who provide care support are paid, for example, while others are not. Of those who are paid, about half are employees of licensed, bonded agencies. The remaining are out-of-pocket cash-paid individuals like neighbors.

By far, the largest group of those providing care support, however, is not paid at all, and many never identify themselves as caregivers. Most often, these are family members, including spouses, life partners, and adult children. Sometimes they are young children who provide care; mostly young preteen and teenage girls who spend on average two and a half hours each school day and four hours each weekend day caregiving. They do such things as helping family members get around, providing emotional support, doing housecleaning and grocery shopping, administering medications, and handling medical equipment.

Even though those who provide care support the recipient's engagement with many of their nonhealth networks, I place this group within the health and vitality network because often it is a health problem, including accidents, injuries, and advanced age, that triggers the need for care support.

Companions are those who provide all types of care support except health care. They do housekeeping chores, food preparation, shopping, transportation, laundry, errands, pet care, and social engagement. People in this care-support role refer to themselves as caregivers or companions interchangeably, but those who are employed by agencies regulated to provide this service are called companions.

Care or case managers are professionals certified to coordinate medical and nonmedical care. They are often nurses or social workers, and within health care, they intervene with physicians, hospitals, other providers, and often with insurance companies to help get what you need. In some cases, they are called navigators and provide information and assistance to link with health care and other social services available in a community.

A care partner is anyone who helps you make major decisions about such matters as health care, household management, downsizing or moving, finances, and legal documents. They may also help with everyday decisions about meal planning, purchases, travel plans, or attending social and community events. Spouses and life partners, adult children, and other close family members are most often care partners, but you might also get this care support from close friends or professional advisers.

Sometimes care partners are also caregivers. Caregivers are those who provide transportation, accompany you to physician visits, or remain with you during hospital stays to assure you get the care you need. They might also accompany you to—or arrange for—meetings with legal and financial or other advisers should you need their help as well. In addition, they help in other ways, including housecleaning, bill paying, laundry, grocery shopping, food preparation, and transportation to church or social gatherings.

The help you receive from those who provide care support, including for life's daily tasks when needed, helps avoid further decline in your health and quality of life. They are essential when you are ill, disabled, very elderly, or recovering from major surgery or an injury. During times like those, the activities of daily living you manage easily can become impossible without assistance.

5. Pet Health and Vitality

These people support your pet's health and vitality. Breeders, rescue organizations, veterinarians and vet technicians, specialists in small and large animal care, kennel staff, groomers, sitters, and walkers are in this group. Other people's pets can be included in this group if your pet attends puppy or kitty kindergarten or day care and if you visit dog parks or have playdates. Also included are those who do special training, including obedience training, assist-animal training, therapy animal training, or search-and-rescue training.

6. Administrative Staff

These people manage administrative operations for those who provide you with health and vitality services, including receptionists, schedulers, billing clerks, insurance specialists, and, in some cases, volunteers. They can be important gatekeepers and worthy of your attention, especially if you or those you care for have serious conditions that require frequent or urgent office visits.

Exploring Your Network

Note those in your health and vitality network today and assure you are connected to a good source of primary care. If needed, assure you have specialist care at a time and place convenient to you. Especially if you must travel for care, assure transportation is available.

Determine if there is someone who can help you navigate the health care system if you suffered an injury or became seriously ill. Determine if you will need to inform your health care providers about friends and family they can contact about your health and whether you will need to sign forms to allow them to do that.

Note whether you have friends, personal trainers, or yoga, dance, or exercise teachers to help you stay fit and whether you have a health and fitness role model, including someone famous and in the public eye or even a fictional character. Note whether you are connected to people who support your healthy lifestyle choices, and if you have a health condition, if they help you manage it well.

How do you feel about your appearance? Ensure you feel confident about the way you look as you engage in work or social activities with others.

If you are caring for the health of a child, spouse, parent, friend, or pet, note whether you have sufficient help to support you so that you can do it well.

Key Points

- This network helps you live a long and healthy life.
- Good health improves personal, family, business, and national wealth.
- A good appearance enhances social standing and economic security.
- Primary health, dental, and vision care are essential.
- Specialist, institutional, and at-home care support are also commonly necessary.

Chapter 6

Education and Enrichment Networks

The Power of Networks in Action

AT THE START OF my career as a school psychologist decades ago, I experienced two vastly different communities, each with different network dynamics. One surrounded a rural school, attended only by old-order Amish children in the area. The boys wore hats; the girls wore bonnets. They came to school in buggies and played barefooted on grassy playgrounds at recess. It was like being in another century, and I never worried about children with special needs at that school. They would grow up within the arms of their families and the even bigger arms of the entire community. They would always have a place and play a role as best they could with the abilities they had. They would not be hampered by stigma or bullied for what they lacked. They would enjoy the dignity each person deserves.

Just twenty miles down the road in the "English" school, however, a child with those same special needs would not be so lucky. They would probably not finish high school and, as adults, would never be more than marginally employed. They would live on the edge of an otherwise solid, middle-class town. They would be bullied at school when they were young and never enter the core life of the community when they matured. It was frustrating to meet a five-year-old and feel we'd already missed the chance to put them on a better life trajectory. This was an era before children with special needs had a legal right to an education, and although they'd win that right eventually, it would be too late for three I will never forget: Chris, Jesse, and Sharon.

Chris was seventeen, living at home, and not in school. In the language of that era, he had been classified as "retarded" by others long before I arrived. No one had noticed that it wasn't lack of intelligence holding him back; it was his hearing. Chris was deaf. Meanwhile, Jesse was ten and not in school either. He had spina bifida, lacked bowel and bladder control, and wore diapers. Sharon was thirteen and in a classroom for children with special needs, with classmates ranging in age from seven to seventeen. She went into labor during class one day, too intellectually limited to be aware she was pregnant or that the child had been fathered by her grandfather.

I was new in town and new on the job. I knew nothing about the human capital within networks or how to leverage it to help these children, and I didn't have any of my own in any case. I was also a newlywed, now living far away from my own family and trying to adjust to my new husband's family network and my career network, all without support of those in my own existing networks hundreds of miles away. It is hard to believe today, but long-distance phone calls were too expensive to be routine and the mail was too slow to be of value. Getting support from my network didn't come easy—or cheap. Luckily, I was working with dedicated educators, and as lifetime residents of the area, they had networks.

Without missing a beat, once they learned about these children, they activated their connections to help. Well-established links between teachers, principals, parents, local business owners, and town leaders made all the difference. Teachers rallied round, willing to learn how to teach children with special needs in their classrooms. Parents formed partnerships to raise funds to supply classrooms with special equipment. Local business clubs contributed to help.

A minister found an elderly couple—both deaf—to train Chris in American sign language. He remained with his family and avoided being sent to a state school more than a hundred miles away. A retired teacher volunteered to homeschool Jesse. A local judge placed Sharon in a foster home, and she returned to school. These children shined a light on others with special needs, and eventually, networks developed and resources expanded to help children with special talents as well. For me, it remains the single most powerful example of how quickly, decisively, and effectively the human capital within a variety of networks can help children achieve their potential to learn.

Network Role and Value

It is the role of those in this network to assure you are educated well as a child and learn what your culture believes are essential facts and skills. If you had special needs, this network should have accommodated those and found ways to help you advance. If you had special talents, this network should have supported you to develop them fully. If yours was a quality network, you progressed to more advanced levels of education or technical skills. Good support from this network helped you explore your unique gifts to the world, develop your abilities, and earn a place in adult society. That helped you find meaningful work, achieve economic well-being, build a good-quality life for yourself and your family, and contribute to the world.

From the moment you were born—and even before that—you learned from the world around you. Early in life, you may have had educational toys or visually interesting mobiles over your crib. You may have attended Mommy and Me classes. Later, your parents or private, parochial, or public schools provided you with a formal education in classrooms. You also had a variety of other enrichment avenues to choose from in your neighborhood or community.

The support of your education and enrichment network did not come solely from teachers, coaches, or other adults, however. The students in your classes and members of your clubs, scout groups, or teams were important too. How well you did academically is related to how well your classmates did, as there are peer effects in school. Even for very young children, fellow students matter. In preschool, for example, if classmates have better language skills, children's language skills improve. After just one year, children who might otherwise struggle because of disabilities gain language skills comparable to children without disabilities when surrounded by highly skilled peers. Your academic success was also influenced by classmates' absenteeism. According to educational psychologist Michael Gottfried at the University of California, Santa Barbara, when some classmates miss school, the entire classroom has lower test scores.

This network provided you with more than factual knowledge. Schools foster social networks, and the relationships created there are important. School gave you the opportunity to make friends, explore nonacademic interests, and learn teamwork in sports. If you did make friends, you were less likely to suffer from anxiety and depression. You were also less likely to be bullied. This is important for everyone but especially for the 40 percent of children who start school without the social skills to develop close friendships and for children with developmental disabilities, who frequently have behavior problems and low social skills. If they have even one best friend, other children accept them.

During my years as an educator, I knew the value of teachers, but I wasn't aware of the data I've just cited about the importance of peers. My friend Terry was aware, however, which was why she asked me and others of our friends to write letters of recommendation to help her four-year-old daughter gain admission to a good school in the city where they lived. As a friend, I was happy to oblige, but at the time, I was not attuned to Terry's rationale until she explained that school exemplified not only a network of good teachers but also good peers. The parents of the other students shared her values for excellence in academics, appreciation of the arts, and ethics in human interactions.

Ensuring her daughter grew up and learned within high-quality peer networks from preschool through high school made Terry's job as a single mom easier. Each day when she left for work—and especially when she traveled out of town for work—she could feel confident that her daughter was in good hands. Terry's instincts about the importance of her child's education network proved right. It made her parenting easier. Her daughter is growing up to be a remarkable young woman, and she will be launched into adult life with vibrant networks to support her aspirations.

A four-year study of ninety thousand high school students provides additional insights about the value of other students. Using a carefully designed method to study the networks of a high school student and up to ten of their close friends, researchers at Brigham Young University found that joining a club or extracurricular activity with members that get the best grades can double the odds of going to college. What's even more interesting, the type of club did not matter. In some schools, students with the best grades were on sports teams or in the school band. In other schools, they ran cross-country or were in the computer club.

This network is one of the key ways in which society transmits its cultural norms, and aside from your family, it is the one in which you spent the most time as a child. Terry very carefully chose the education network she wanted for her daughter and found a perfect match. Not every parent and child is able to do that. If you were someone who did not align with the norm in your behavior, abilities, or identity, it may not have supported you. If your gender, gender identity, race, ethnicity, special needs, or special talents did not fit with society or the school at the time, your experiences may have been unsupportive and even harmful.

Relatively recent work on the value of diversity and multiple intelligences has enlightened us, but even today most schools are not structured to recognize and reward any more than typical middle-class behavior and traditional reading, writing, and arithmetic of the three Rs. If you were distractible, overly energetic, or not talented in those three subject areas, you may not have received the support you deserved. Even if you were talented in areas the world needs, you may not have been recognized for that and nurtured by teachers to hone those skills.

A study by educational psychologist Dr. John R. Rader demonstrated that clearly. Rader selected six people known for the important contributions they made to the world and gathered their elementary school records. Some were historical figures, and no actual records were available, so he created some using biographical accounts. He included information about their genetics, physical health, intellectual abilities, family relationships, social skills, emotional maturity, and goals in life. Then he labeled each record with a fictitious name.

I was in graduate school at the time and helped him gather the data. We assembled groups of parents, teachers, and principals and asked them to review the six records and select two for a special program for talented children. Each person made selections individually, and then the group arrived at a consensus about the final choices. Then we revealed the real identities of the children, and everyone learned who they'd chosen and who they'd rejected.

People in Rader's study passed over Abraham Lincoln because he lacked family, economic, and social advantages, and had a genetic condition—Marfan syndrome—known to shorten life span. They didn't select Eleanor Roosevelt because she was shy and withdrawn, her father was an alcoholic, and her stated life goal—to help people—was "soft." Dancer Isadora Duncan rated low because the arts, generally, were not valued.

Who did educators prefer? They selected children with more traditional skills. One was a boy who completed a mathematics PhD in his teens. The other was Bill Bradley. He was not yet a US senator but had already demonstrated his academic abilities as a Rhodes scholar and his athletic talent as a professional basketball player.

If you are one of those held back, disadvantaged in your childhood, or were like the notables in Radar's study who did not fit the mold traditional educational institutions expect, those biases no longer control your destiny. As an adult, opportunities to express your talent or learn new skills are just a few mouse clicks away. You can get access to audiences, teachers, and peers more easily now than ever before. You can explore education and enrichment experiences on any subject from anywhere in the world. Your options for exploring the arts, sciences, technology, and humanities are no longer confined by your past, your location, or your finances. They are endless.

Inside Education and Enrichment Networks

I organize this network into two different groups, those who support *education* to prepare you for the workplace and those who support *enrichment* regardless of your age or career stage.

1. Education

These people provide you with your formal education in schools, including those who teach general subjects and those who specialize in subjects like math, music, art, or physical education. Also included are individual tutors, classroom aides, and those who work in advanced or remedial education. Not everyone in an education network is engaged directly with students in classrooms. Experts in administration— principals, superintendents, and specialists like guidance counselors and speech and language therapists—are involved as well. Schools are supported by parent-teacher associations or home and school associations, as well as by employed staff or contractors who provide bus transportation, food services, playground monitoring, and security. Included in this network are other students and classroom peers who are participants in school clubs, sports, and other activities.

Formal education begins as early as pre-K in programs like Bright Futures, Head Start, Montessori, or day care programs. This network then advances through kindergarten, elementary school, middle school, high school, and college. It can also include graduate or professional schools in specialized programs like medicine, engineering, or law. Formal education can advance even further within various highly specialized fields through residencies, fellowships, and clerkships. This is the network that prepares you for the work world or, as a retiree, satisfies your need for lifelong learning or your desire to earn an advanced degree even if you are at an advanced age.

2. Enrichment

These people provide you with learning opportunities outside of the formal, school day settings, including those who guide art, music, or dance instruction. In some cases, these people staff programs offered before or after the formal school day and may include childcare to support working parents. Included in school-based enrichment of this type are those who supervise and participate in school newspaper or yearbook clubs, sports teams, computer clubs, language clubs, and school music or theater production groups.

Enrichment programs are common outside of educational institutions as well, and you can engage with people in any one of your networks to pursue them. Music instructors teach in their homes or studios. Local sports leagues provide opportunities for people of all ages. Public library staff and volunteers offer storytelling sessions. Museum staff and volunteer docents offer individual and group tours. Private studios hold classes in needlework, pottery, photography, and bonsai. Writers groups and culinary clubs form as collaborative efforts of the people involved and sometimes as classes led by experts. Senior centers have classes in art, music, dance, investing, and computer use. Churches arrange trips to theaters and sports events.

Exploring Your Network

Reflect on your school years growing up and identify memories that stand out because of the people involved, noting teachers, coaches, or classmates, and how connections with them created a lasting influence.

Take special note of whether you had special needs or special talents that were honored and accommodated and whether that impacts you today.

Consider how before- or after-school programs or school clubs allowed you to pursue your interests and how they helped you create the life you have today.

If you changed schools often because you were in foster care or your parents were in the military or relocated for their jobs, note the impact on enduring friendships and academic achievement.

Recall parents, teachers, or mentors who introduced you to the arts or gave you the opportunity to sing, dance, or play a musical instrument. Recall whether you could visit museums and art institutes and were encouraged to explore your own talents.

As an adult, explore educational, artistic, or other enrichment programs available through your workplace, local colleges and universities, or community and consider how they will not only be intellectually rewarding but also help you satisfy other needs, including for social engagement or spiritual connections.

Key Points

- This network assures you learn the facts and skills valued by society.
- It fosters social network connections and transmits social norms, disadvantaging those who do not conform.
- Not just teachers but also fellow students have an impact on social and academic success in school.
- Modern technology and global communications support increasingly available personal education and enrichment opportunities for people of all ages.
- This network supports social and community network connections, which benefit people of all ages.

Chapter 7
Spiritual Networks

Missing Peace

MARIAN AND VINCE HAD known each other in high school but attended different universities, married college sweethearts, and lived in different towns many miles apart. Their spouses succumbed to cancer, and they were both widowed when they reconnected at a high school reunion. The rest is history, as they say, and they married soon after.

Both had children from their previous marriages, but none of them lived at home. Two were in college, one was in law school, and a fourth was married and expecting a baby. As empty nesters, they could downsize both family homes and relocate to a condo midway between their jobs to share the commute.

It wasn't until she explored her networks that Marian realized that the important connections they had with others—especially in their spiritual lives—had fallen by the wayside. In her words, "I was always active in my church, and it was a special source of support for me when my husband died. Vince got support from people in his church as well. When we moved away, we did more than leave neighbors and friends. We left the connections we had with people in our churches behind too. With all the excitement of falling in love again, a wedding, and the work of relocating, I didn't have time to notice that I had disconnected from rich spiritual traditions and all the people who were so helpful during those tough times."

There was more. "In part, I think it happened because we didn't have kids at home," Marian went on. "When kids are around, you think about everything you want to teach them, and that includes the spiritual side of life. As a parent, you also need lots of help and want the social support a congregation provides to families. Maybe if our kids had been younger, we would have remained connected to our church." The NetworkSage road map showed Marian the missing part of her life and helped her learn she and Vince had lost an important connection they wanted to restore. Eventually, she and Vince connected with a congregation in their new town, and that brought them the sense of peace they wanted for their new stage of life.

Network Role and Value

Marian was right about the challenges of relocating and the role of children in connecting parents to networks, including those of formal spiritual congregations. As more people remain single, relocate often, and live longer without children at home, many in the United States today are disconnecting from traditional network supports, including formal religious networks. Where spirituality is concerned, they are finding new, more informal spiritual connections or are going it alone.

Those factors add to already growing trends toward secularization that happened as people departed from the traditions of their parents. Religious intermarriage was already well under way, and most religions adapted to mixed-marriage families, which helped. Rejection of religious traditions altogether, however, is relatively new and is hard on some people. Joanne, for example, is conservative on religious matters and has not come to peace with her grown children's secular or "spiritual, not religious" approach to life and their rejection of what they learned when they were young. She believes her grandchildren are missing religious training they should have. She misses the milestone rituals she wanted them to experience. Her heart aches that they may never understand the deeper meanings of the holidays they celebrate. This creates tensions between her and her children, and she fears those will worsen as her grandchildren grow up. She also doubts her children's claim that being spiritual can fill the void of religion lost. Joanne may someday learn whether that is so since, as noted a Pew Research Center study, an increasing number of people report that they have no religious affiliation at all, and those who say they are "spiritual but not religious" now outnumber the country's largest church-affiliated group: Catholics.

This network supports humankind's search for meaning, particularly in the face of difficult times and inexplicable events. As chronicled so well by writer and lecturer Joseph Campbell in his work on comparative mythology and religion, this search involved practices of indigenous cultures and today's major world religions. These practices marked the hours of the day, the seasons of the year, and the milestones of life, all with different prayers and rituals. These shared experiences within families and communities bonded people with one another and with the divine. They helped humankind cope with the seemingly unknowable, uncontrollable forces that threatened survival. Their founders, exemplars, and saints were models of the personal characteristics that their traditions admired and attempted to emulate.

It is the role of this network to help you learn your religion's canons, ethics, and codes of behavior. It teaches you how to worship and express its values through study and appropriate behavior toward other people and the divine. If you practice within a religious congregation today and it supports you well, you feel a strong sense of community and experience the best expressions of its beliefs. It helps you celebrate the milestones of your life. You receive its care, compassion, and charity when you need it. If it does not support you—particularly when you face a life crisis—you can feel alienated from the tradition, betrayed by the community, and even abandoned by the divine. If you do not feel welcome, you can feel shunned and shamed.

All the world's religious traditions recommend spiritual practices to a greater or lesser degree, but spirituality and religion need not be a joint venture. Some people practice their religion but engage in no other spiritual endeavors. Others maintain spiritual practices without being connected to a formal religious tradition. Spiritual practices are those that help develop your sense of presence, awareness, mindfulness, compassionate caring, and appreciation of the arts or practice of ethics. They can also involve studying, bearing witness to suffering, tending to the poor, and protecting vulnerable people, animals, or the environment. Cultivating gratitude and beauty can be a spiritual practice as are the ancient and nearly universal practices of connecting with nature, walking a labyrinth, chanting, or drumming. Yoga, meditation, journaling, or certain forms of psychotherapy can be spiritual practices as can be a chosen career or parenting style.

Religion and spirituality—an important factor in human development and transformation—is, today, undergoing transformation as well. Global communication, travel, and immigration give you easy access to all the world's religious, spiritual, and insight traditions. It is also likely that you have more leisure time than earlier generations to learn about them and determine if they are valuable for your own life and human development. Importantly, in many nations, you have more social and political freedom to do so.

This freedom is not absolute, however, and some people find that personal spiritual practices are not without consequences within some religious congregations. Judy was a longtime client who attended a church for many years before developing an interest in yoga that blossomed into a personal daily practice. Others in her congregation noticed a change in her and remarked on her new state of calm and equanimity. Without realizing it would create a controversy, she told them she credited yoga for her newfound sense of peace. In fact, she even suggested that the church consider offering classes in one of their activity rooms and volunteered to connect the pastor with her yoga teacher.

Initially, the church leaders politely refused her offer. Over time, however, they became hostile not only to her suggestion but to her personal practice. They asserted that yoga was the religion and inconsistent with their theology. She felt pressured to quit yoga, but it was subtle, and she valued her relationships with the congregation, so she decided to stop talking about her private practices. As an added incentive for her silence, she and her husband were raising their children in that church, so keeping the peace by avoiding a controversy about yoga felt wise.

The breaking point came several months later when Judy and her husband attended a weekend retreat at a well-known yoga center in Massachusetts. He learned to meditate, and before long, his high blood pressure returned to normal, and he coped better with stress at work. He gave the credit to the meditation practice. Unfortunately, when he talked about these benefits at a church prayer group meeting, some people who overheard him became alarmed. They didn't wait to talk with him privately; they spoke out, warning him that meditation allowed demons to enter someone's mind.

Both Judy and her husband benefitted from their practices of yoga and meditation, and now the pressure to quit was no longer subtle and couldn't be justified. After months of talking and more than a few tears, they left their church and found another place to raise their children within a religious congregation that was more accepting of the personal practices they valued.

Inside Spiritual Networks

I organize this network into two groups, those who support your life in *religious congregations* and in your *personal spirituality*.

1. Religious Congregations

The people in your religious congregation include the leaders of churches, synagogues, or mosques. They are pastors, ministers, priests, deacons, rabbis, mohels, imams, and others who lead services, retreats, and special celebrations. As leaders, these people play a special role in major life milestones, including baptisms, bris ceremonies, coming-of-age rituals like First Communions, Confirmations, Quinceañeras, Bar Mitzvahs and Bat Mitzvahs, Upanayana (a Hindu coming-of-age Sacred Thread ceremony), and weddings and funerals.

Religious congregations include church members as well as those who support the leadership and congregation as employed staff or volunteers, including parish councils, cantors, choirs, choir directors, presbytery and religious education teachers. Others in this group include children's godparents or youth ministers, program directors, and retreat leaders.

Some congregations provide special childcare, elder care, health care, and mental health care services not only for their members but for others in the community as well. When they do, those who are employed or who volunteer their services as teachers, therapists, and care providers are part of this network.

Zen is not, strictly speaking, a religion or religious community, but it shares features common to religious congregations. Like leaders of other communities, Zen masters have completed a course of study and lead the community—called a *sangha*—instructing Zen students and presiding over rituals and milestone life events. A Zen temple or a *zendo* is the community's spiritual home and is staffed by paid employees and volunteers and may provide a variety of social services and charitable works for its members and for others in the world.

2. Personal Spirituality

These people provide teachings and experiences of a spiritual nature outside of any formal religious congregation. Included here are workshop leaders, authors, televangelists, yoga instructors, meditation teachers, and spiritual directors. Also included are friends or organizations with whom you engage in any practice that supports your spiritual growth, including volunteer work or being in nature.

The founder or exemplar of your religion might also be in your personal spiritual group if you feel a deep and special kinship with him or her—as Christians might feel toward Jesus or a saint, or as Hindus might feel for Krishna or Durga. If so, they have a place within this group. If you feel deeply connected to one of today's accessible spiritual teachers or writers—His Holiness the Dali Lama, Pema Chŏdrŏn, or Deepak Chopra, for example—they would be included. Also included can be a career coach if your chosen profession is an expression of your personal spirituality, or your psychotherapist if you pursue therapy to develop your spiritually.

Some people say that all people are intimately and ultimately connected to one another, and if you are one of them, your own spiritual group might be so expansive as to include all other people and even all sentient beings. People who feel this way often express it through loving-kindness meditation—also called Metta meditation—which extends well wishes to other people individually and, eventually, to all beings.

Exploring Your Network

Recall the spiritual network your parents created for you within—or outside of—one of the major religious traditions of the world and note what you learned from them, either from their teaching or from their examples.

Consider your rationale as you chose to stay or leave that tradition and determine the impact that had on all your networks.

Recall times people in this network provided you with counsel or comfort during times of crises and whether, if you suffered a crisis, you would have the support of this network today.

Determine if those in your care—an elderly parent or seriously ill friend—want spiritual support that you can help facilitate.

Key Points

- This network supports humankind's search for meaning and solace, especially in the face of events that threaten survival.
- Disconnecting from religious congregations is a relatively new and growing trend.
- The number of people in the United States who say they are "spiritual, not religious" outnumbers any single religious group.
- Modern technology and global communications support access to all the world's religious and spiritual traditions.

Chapter 8

Social and Community Networks

Tupperware Triage

CHERYL WAS EXTROVERTED AND wonderfully funny and had a big social network. Many of her friends had home-based, socially networked businesses. That meant invitations to parties for Tupperware, jewelry, cooking, stamping, and kitchen gadgets. She loved her friends, she loved their parties, and her packed-to-the-brim schedule was never a problem. She left each one energized and looked forward to more.

Then life dealt her a wild card. Cheryl left a corporate job to start a consulting firm, and not long after, her mother was hospitalized in a distant city. Her husband helped, but starting a new business, being a wife, and managing long-distance caregiving didn't leave her time to attend parties. As a NetworkSage, she soon understood it was creating far more stress than she could manage well. She needed to build a successful business, didn't want to ignore her husband, couldn't walk away from her mother's needs, and wanted to support her friends' businesses.

It was her mother's illness that stretched her beyond her capacity, and it didn't take long for her to see she'd fallen into an old pattern. Like most people, without being consciously aware of it, she was starting to cheat on sleep and self-care to support the important people in her

95

family, career, and social networks. Refocusing on all her networks showed her a better way through. She sent a note to the friends in her social network saying, "I love you, and I want to support your business. But here's the deal: I've got a lot happening in my life right now, and as much as I'd like to, I don't have the time to come to each party. Until the dust settles: I can come to one. You pick the day, and I will be there."

With that note, she set a boundary to have the time and energy to build her business, have quality time with her husband, care for her mom, and support her friends. Eventually, her mom recovered, and she reengaged with her friends more often and in all the ways she enjoyed.

Network Role and Value

It is the role of this network to help you move safely and easily outside your family home to engage with others in the wider world. It helps you get access to goods, services, and social experiences you cannot provide for yourself. If this network supports you well, you encounter new people, have a diversity of enriching opportunities, and build relationships that endure.

This is the network that supports for public health measures like clean water, safe streets, access to healthy food, places to play, parks to enjoy, and affordable housing. It provides you with good highways, mass transit, and opportunities to be engaged as a citizen in good governance. This network also allows you to contribute to community endeavors to improve life for yourself and others in your town, which you may have done even as a child, learning leadership skills that serve you well today. I did this through Girl Scouts. My pre–Title IX childhood did not give girls access to sports, and gender limitations imposed on girls at school was an accepted way of life. Girl Scouts gave girls opportunities to volunteer, support others in town, practice teamwork, and learn leadership when other networks didn't.

The composition of your social and community network changes over the course of your lifetime. When you were a child, this network may have been limited to the neighbors in your apartment building or a small playgroup arranged by your parents. Later, it expanded to include your entire neighborhood, the friends of your siblings, and your friends at scouts, school, or in sports. In high school—especially when you could drive or use mass transit and be independent of your parents—it grew to include one of the many service clubs or school groups you could join.

As an adult, this group expands even more. Your social and community network today might include not only your friends—including friends at work—but also those who are friends of family members and those who are friends of friends. It might also include those in your neighborhood, town, state, or nation. In fact, you might be involved in global ventures and include people from other nations in your community. Today's global media, inexpensive communication technologies, social media, and affordable air travel facilitate a global mind-set like no other time in history.

What you need from this network changes over time as well. As a child, you needed adults in this network to assure you were safe but also to help you learn responsible ways of being with others outside your family. As a teen, you needed places to gather with friends that offered you some autonomy but also protected you against impulsive actions that could harm you or others. As a parent, you need affordable childcare. If you have a disabling condition, you need access to buildings that accommodate you. As an older adult, you may need ready access to services like public transportation, safe places to exercise, and affordable housing to help you age well in place.

Beginning in your teens (and certainly now as an adult), the number of people you counted as connections in this network mattered, especially if those numbers were on the high side. After all, being known and liked socially got you elected to student council, votes for prom queen, blind dates, and niche friends to help satisfy your love of everything from baseball to Bach. Eventually, these friends used their networks to help you find internships, a job, and an apartment in a new town. Social media sites like Facebook, Twitter, and LinkedIn upped the ante and helped you find friends from times past, enlarging your social and community network even more.

At some point in life, however, the metrics change. As life gets complicated, or your needs change, you may need to limit the size of this network or shift the types of connections you have. If you travel during the week because of your job, you may need to limit social engagements and volunteering to weekends. As you have children, you may choose to limit leadership in community organizations in favor of volunteering at your child's school. In fact, becoming a parent can cause radical shifts in your social and community network. It is common for parents to lose touch with their friends, which is a risk factor for perinatal depression. If you own a home, you may find maintenance and renovations are too time-consuming to allow you to star in a community theater production. Or, conversely, now that you have a home, you may connect with others more frequently as you entertain, host the block party at your place, or allow a local club to add your property for their annual fundraising garden walk.

If you change your life's goals, it is likely your social and community network connections will change too. That was the case for one college sophomore who told me, "They say that in college you can do two of these three things: study, sleep, or socialize. In my freshman year, I didn't sleep. This year, I could see how foolish it was to be sleep-deprived all the time. Looking carefully at networks helped me see where to cut back." She divided her friends into four different groups based on how close she felt to them and cut back on contacts with the lowest priority group so she could nurture friendships in her new sorority, study, and finally get some sleep.

If you marry, social connections change, and if a marriage ends, friendships split up as well. This happened to Josh, who wasn't yet married but had been dating someone as he worked in his first job in a new town. "Social life? What social life? I dated this girl for six months, and when it ended, she walked away with all my friends. I decided I'd never let that happen again. I see now how friends can change when you have a major event in your life. I thought that only happened to divorced people. I thought they were the only ones whose friends picked sides."

If you retire, social networks can change dramatically. Retirement relocation looked enticing for one colleague who was happy about being able to be near her children and grandchildren, until she learned she would need to rebuild her entire social life. "I looked at my network lists, and it made me wonder: How would I ever replace the friends I made in my jobs and my neighborhood? How would I find people now that I'm not working?" A recent retiree, Richard, made a similar observation, even though he did not have relocation plans. "I had no idea how much of my social life revolved around my career," he told me. "In fact, a lot of my life did. Not only did my job satisfy my career aspirations, give me a good income and a sense of purpose, at work, I could socialize. When I retired, I lost a lot more than a desk and an office."

The death of a spouse changes social and community networks as well, some of which are unexpected, as I learned from a recently widowed friend. "When my husband was alive, we enjoyed dinner and theater with other couples. Now that he is gone, our friends are welcoming, and they include me, but it does not feel the same. It feels less like friendship and more like charity, so I prefer to be with other widows and singles."

Inside Social and Community Networks

I organize this network into three groups, those in your *personal social life*, your *community-wide engagement*, and your *virtual social life*.

1. Personal Social Life

Your own personal social life includes your friends, neighbors, workplace friends, and friends with whom you enjoy special interests like music, sports, or hobbies—or perhaps, as my widowed friend taught me, someone you enjoy doing nothing with. If you are dating, at some stage in any courtship, that person's friends, colleagues, and eventually family members will be included. When you have a spouse or life partner, that person's family, friends, and colleagues are part of your network. If you have children, your children's friends and their parents are included, as are friends of your parents and siblings.

If you have elderly parents, their friends can be included on your list, especially if you think you may need their assistance at some point in the future. The value of this hit home in a discussion with an East Coast colleague. Her former mother-in-law lived in the Midwest and recently had a serious auto accident. This colleague's daughter lived in a neighboring town and rushed to be at her grandmother's hospital bedside for several days. Staying at her grandmother's home each evening, my colleague's daughter searched without success to find information about her grandmother's friends so she could inform them and engage their support. Web searches and 411 calls were also unsuccessful. Finally, she thought to call the local Methodist church where her grandmother had been a lifelong congregant. That succeeded in finding friends at the church who, in turn, knew other friends who then became the source of support her grandmother needed as she returned home to recover.

2. Community Social Life

Community social life includes engagement with nearby neighborhoods and, in addition, with structured collaborations through community organizations. Some are advocacy groups that promote policies to support the needs of others, like children, the disabled, the elderly, veterans, animals, and the environment. Others provide services, caring for those in need of food, shelter, education, and social support, or engaging in projects to beautify community surroundings. Some promote music, theater, art, dance, and other cultural events, while others organize as political parties or for nonpartisan political action. Still others are committed to supporting children and youth with after-school programs, clubs, or sports.

If you are engaged in your community, your network will include the leaders, volunteers, participants, beneficiaries, and funders of these various community-wide groups. For example, if you are a Little League or soccer coach, your network includes those in league leadership, umpires, playing-field managers, players, parents, competitor team coaches, and fans. If the team does well, this number can expand during tournaments to include local media too.

3. Virtual Social Life

Social media connections can never replace the real face-to-face human connections you need, but they can serve some needs you have and are valuable for that reason. Dating sites allow you to arrange introductions and progress through several stages of courtship virtually. Facebook, Twitter, Instagram, and Pinterest help you to create broadly based social networks by finding old friends and keeping pace with their lives. Social media allows you to communicate with friends efficiently, and though there is more to your social needs than just communication, it's a good place to start. That is especially true if your life changes and gets more complicated, you relocate away from friends and family, or you travel often for work. It is also true if you are deployed in the military, become ill or disabled, or for other reasons are unable to easily venture away from home.

Social media also allows you to connect with like-minded people to pursue social and political action and to get help when you need it. A parent up nights with a colicky baby, for example, will get support and advice more quickly from a Facebook parent group than the child's pediatric office. It is a way for friends to share experiences or for anyone to crowd-source tips, as seniors do more frequently these days about retirement and living independently.

iPhones, iPads, Androids, laptops, desktops, and other smart devices help you create a virtual social life. Although these are tools that connect you to others, you connect to these devices and, increasingly, in ways that mirror connections with people. Losing one—or being denied the opportunity to use it—can create the same symptoms as withdrawing from addictive substances or being shunned by a social group. If that is the case for you, it may be time to count your devices along with the human connections in your networks. This is particularly true if, like so many people today, you prioritize your devices ahead of the real people in your life. Doing so will help you decide if adjusting your priorities might be necessary.

Exploring Your Network

Recall your earliest social and community networks, their distinctive characteristics, the features you most enjoyed, and how that helps shapes this network in your life today.

Describe how this network changed as you became older, progressed through school, could drive, attended college, got a job, or married, noticing which friendships drifted apart and how you made new connections with others you met along the way.

Determine the role of social media in your life, whether actively engaging there supports the quality of connections you want and need.

If you plan to divorce, relocate, retire, or live independently as a senior, consider how that will change this network and determine how you will maintain supportive connections—or build new ones—to prevent loneliness and isolation.

If you have older relatives—even if you are not responsible for their well-being—determine if they are socially connected and encourage them to maintain good social connections as a key to healthy aging.

Key Points

- This network helps you move safely and easily as you engage in the world outside your family.
- It grows larger as you grow, encompassing friends, friends of friends, and people in distant places.
- It changes as other networks and life stages or life events change, shrinking or growing as your needs require.
- You need face-to-face engagement with real people. Social media engagement in a virtual world is not sufficient for health, well-being, and success.

Chapter 9

Career Networks

Carl's Clarity

CARL LEFT A MAJOR law firm to start his own practice and was the first NetworkSage attorney. He began his exploration with his career network, naming each client and all the attorneys and support staff who had joined the firm since its founding.

It would be months before he'd return to explore his other networks because of his big reveal after just twenty minutes. That's when he stopped to call me to say he could not manage the firm he had built and deliver the value he wanted to the three hundred clients who depended on him personally.

He set goals to get management help and to pare his client list to just thirty—big ones. Focusing on his list, he identified his top clients and created a new roster. He took his smaller clients to dinner, told them he could not give them the attention they deserved, and referred them to other attorneys he trusted to help them better.

Two months later, he called again, this time to say he was making more money and playing more golf and that his wife was happier too. That was Carl's definition of satisfaction and success. I couldn't have been happier for him.

Network Role and Value

It is the role of the people in this network to support you as you express your talents and achieve your aspirations in the work world. If it supports you well, you will build economic security for yourself and your family, make meaningful contributions to the world, and feel satisfied with your accomplishments. This network has changed dramatically in the past several decades as women have entered the workforce, as workweeks and working years have expanded, as technology has changed the nature of work, and as we've attempted to balance work with other parts of life.

If you have come of age and are creating a career network, the strengths and weaknesses of all your other networks will show up now in full force. All your other networks matter now more than ever because every connection you have in any of your other networks can help—or harm—your career prospects and advancement.

If people in other networks have supported you well, you are prepared for the work world. You are healthy, well educated, and happily involved socially. You have a good family life, a supportive group of friends, and perhaps a spirituality that infuses your work with meaning and helps you to be resilient when times are tough. Your family, health providers, friends, neighborhood, and religious congregation make allowances for the demands of your job. If you are a parent working outside your home, your network connections will not expect you to play the social role of one who does not. They won't be critical if you hire a housekeeper, decline to host Thanksgiving dinner, or limit volunteering to requests from your child's school. If you have a job that requires you to work different shifts and be available for emergencies or as a substitute, others will be accommodating when you need to make last-minute changes.

Support from other networks also means *your* connections will activate *their* connections to help advance your career goals, whether you are building a résumé to find a job, moving up in the ranks of an organization, or building a client list to succeed in a business you own. Each connection in any network is a potential ally to help make that happen, not only at the start of your career but at each step along the way.

One friend's experience is an example. "My kids' dentist knows that I am a marketing consultant, and given where we live, there are lots of prospective clients among the families he sees. He asked for my résumé in case he met anyone in need of my services." In this case, someone from her children's health and vitality network is supporting her career. I have other examples too. Time and again, I'd brainstorm with clients about people in their networks who could help them succeed on a project that bedeviled them. In nearly all cases, they had already reviewed lists of people in their company, consultants they knew, and others in their field without much luck. When I suggested they consider people in other networks, like tennis partners, running buddies, congregation members, or other soccer parents, they always found several who held the key to success.

Optimizing the value of the human capital in other networks is vitally important in today's volatile workplaces. It is difficult to advance, for example, if your noncareer networks are large, difficult to manage, not supportive, or lack important resources you need. It might seem mundane, but consider the value of having a reliable, trustworthy plumber in your home and personal affairs network that day you discover a leak as you head out the door for a flight or an important client meeting. Having a good one will reduce the stress you feel as you leave your home in his hands, meet your career obligations, and protect your standing in your workplace.

Robust networks are more important today than ever before, since employment stability and career-path certainty of times past are disappearing rapidly. Lifetime work with a single employer is no longer a reality and, for younger generations, no longer valued. Even within companies, fewer jobs come with clear command-and-control, process-heavy hierarchies that demand compliance and grant rewards or guarantee future employment. More often, power and decision-making are distributed across teams and work groups. Project success depends on the ability to work autonomously but also collaboratively, negotiating every step of the way. It can be exciting and rewarding but also demanding because of the management challenges involved.

This is also important because of the many people working outside companies, engaged in an important shift in workforce dynamics called the "gig" economy. In the gig economy, people are engaged by companies as independent contractors for short-term assignments. Technology, increasingly mobile workers, millennials' values, and, more recently, non-employment-based health insurance helped make that happen. It is a growing trend in the economy, and Intuit predicts that by 2020, just a few short years from now, 40 percent of US workers will be involved as 1099 independent contractors rather than W-2 employees.

Regardless of your workplace, and whether you are an employee or the business owner, quality connections will enhance your success. Other people can help you learn about opportunities for advancement and act as the sounding board, mentor, or champion. They can introduce you to new clients, prospective jobs, or contracting opportunities. They will connect you to others you don't know who will have information that is not already available to you. Manage connections out beyond your immediate circle of friends, and you can expand your horizons and, as you do, build your reputation and opportunities for the future.

Inside Career Networks

I organize this network into four groups that support your role in the work world: *employment, career networking, career education,* and *career transition*.

1. Employment

These are the people you engage in your workplace or career whether you are an employee or independent contractor. The size and nature of this on-the-job network depends on the type of work you do, but in general, all jobs involve connections with two major groups of people: those within your workplace, like bosses and colleagues, and those outside of it, like customers and clients. These similarities apply to small and large organizations, independent contractors, and throughout the profit, nonprofit, and government sectors. It applies if you work from home on your dining room table or if you commute to an office in a distant city.

In a traditional, company-based job, this group includes a boss or supervisor and, for most people, peers and subordinates. In addition, you may connect with your boss's boss, your supervisor's supervisor, or ranking executives and their executive secretaries. If you have a managerial-level position, you may have an administrative assistant and your own direct reports, and *their* direct reports may be included in this group.

Your workplace group might also include colleagues in other functional areas that support your job or the organization's mission. These would be the people in research and development, manufacturing, marketing, sales, corporate affairs, and business development. People in investor relations, human resources, accounting and finance, information technology, legal and regulatory, and facilities management might be included in this group as well, particularly if you work in a large organization. If you have a leadership role, the board of directors or trustees may be part of this group. If your workplace is a small organization, many of these same people may be vendors rather than employees.

Outside your workplace, your career network can include customers, clients, or constituents. In addition, you may be engaged with financial institution executives, government regulators, tax and license authority officials, the press and citizen or other special interest groups, product distributors, and business brokers. If you are involved in collaborative ventures or partnerships with other organizations, the people in those organizations and their customers, clients, and constituents become a part of your career network too.

2. Career Networking

These are the people and groups you engage to advance your career goals by connecting with others professionally. If you work in a large organization, you may have access to internal networking groups, which are sometimes organized to support the needs of special groups of employees: women, minorities, new hires, or interns, for example. You might also use virtual career platforms created by LinkedIn, Facebook, and Twitter.

If you work in an industry or profession with local, regional, national, and international membership associations, those create network opportunities as well. If you are an entrepreneur or join membership organizations like the Chamber of Commerce or special affinity groups, you have network options as a member. These organizations host social events and offer ways to raise your visibility, grow your reputation, and demonstrate your leadership skills on committees and boards and to show your expertise as a presenter at conferences.

3. Career Education

Your education and enrichment network gave you the skills to qualify for your career. In an evolving workforce economy, it is likely that your skills must evolve as well, and this is the group that helps you adapt and succeed.

When you're hired as an employee, your new boss, colleagues, human resources personnel, or company orientation staff teach you about the company and its policies and procedures. You might also be oriented to the position by your supervisor or someone who previously held that post. During your career, you may be given developmental assignments in temporary positions or in cross-functional work teams, which are not only robust learning opportunities but also new connection opportunities. When you're hired as a consultant, your client and the company's contracting, legal, and accounts payable departments will orient you to their policies and procedures.

You can also receive continuing education from on-the-job trainers, career-development course leaders, and workshop leaders. In some jobs and professions, continuing education is considered so important to maintaining and improving skills that government regulations, licensing organizations, and credentialing agencies require it. Even if your job does not require continuing education, new knowledge and skills are necessary to keep pace with the explosion of technology and information available today. People in this group can be selected by your employer, but you can engage help on your own if you believe special seminar leaders, business coaches, consultants, productivity experts, or local college coursework will improve your prospects for advancement.

4. Career Transition

These people assist you in making career transitions. Former coworkers and employers are included in this group as well as others in your noncareer networks. Former teachers, career coaches, life coaches, and recruiters are included here, as are those who edit résumés, refine LinkedIn profiles, and check your background for prospective employers.

If your career transition involves relocating, you may need assistance from friends, colleagues, educators, realtors, and relocation specialists as you make the decision, and then later as you make the move. If you relocate outside the United States, you will also need attorneys and tax advisers to understand the impact of income generated overseas and how that nation's work laws will determine whether your spouse or life partner can be employed. If you have children, you'll need help from experts who understand different educational systems to make the best school choice. You and your family may also need language tutors or advisers to ensure you are culturally sensitive and behave appropriately.

If your transition is not voluntary, you may need legal services, and since long transitions can have an impact on your financial and mental well-being, you may also need assistance from debt, financial, and tax advisers, state unemployment agency personnel, and mental health therapists. If your transition involves retirement, you may need advice from other retirees, retirement counselors, workshop leaders, and legal and financial advisers to build plans for your next stage of life.

Exploring Your Network

Thinking about your career, note who inspired you to pursue it, whether it was different from others in your birthright networks, and whether you feel supported by them in what you do today.

Determine if there are opportunities in this network to find mentors, sponsors, and supportive networks and if someone in this network will help you find jobs, advanced career opportunities, or customers for your business.

If you are in a service business, a nonprofit or social service provider, assure there are ways you support yourself and your team as you work to address the unmet—and sometimes seemingly insurmountable— needs of those you serve.

If your career does not satisfy or reward you, you are considering a career move, or are working in a rapidly evolving field, determine if you are connected to people who can advise and support you or refer you to others who can.

If you are contemplating retirement, list those in your networks who can help you understand and plan for this major life transition, including those you know who are models of retirement living who can teach you what they have learned.

Key Points

- This network supports you as you express your talents and achieve career aspirations.
- It helps you build new skills and economic security.
- Success in this network is impacted by the strengths and weaknesses of other networks.
- Changes in today's workplaces require greater self-management of career and other networks.

Chapter 10

Home and Personal Affairs Network

An (Almost) Mountain Cabin

KEVIN WAS THE FOUNDER of a technology business that was growing well. He and his wife had three children and appreciated their lifestyle in the mountains of the far Northwest. They found a school that matched their values, with good teachers and enlightened administrators, and like most parents, they formed friendships with other families through the school and the children's sports.

When we met, they had just signed the papers to purchase a new home, and Kevin was buried in business matters while squeezing in a long list of new-home inspections before the deal closed. He was also adapting to the longer commute to this new home in the country and to moose visits (yes, moose!) at the kitchen window.

That's not all. His family was considering buying a vacation cabin with several others. They all got along well, there was a nice mix of boys and girls, and they shared similar interests for outdoor adventures. Some weeks would be allocated to each family, and others would be set aside so they could all vacation together. It sounded great to everyone, especially the kids.

As we talked, Kevin saw the challenges that lay ahead. Like everyone who sees their networks for the first time, he was surprised at the complexity of the life he'd built. He had a growing business, a larger home, and a longer commute. His new house would need some work, and the moose would need watching. Finding the time and energy to find, purchase, and maintain a vacation home that was also a joint business venture with three other families would be challenging. Even under the best of circumstances, it was more a demanding management load than he had imagined. He and his wife decided against it.

Network Role and Value

Kevin and his wife went from being single people to being married, parents, owners of a starter home, owners of a bigger home, and—almost—owners of a timeshare cabin with friends, all while Kevin was managing a rapidly growing business. Even if your life has not progressed at Kevin's pace, as an adult, you assume responsibilities, acquire assets, and have personal affairs to manage. It is the role of people in this network to help you as you do.

If they support you well, you will have greater confidence and peace of mind. You will make good decisions about which assets—like homes and cars—to buy to have the quality of life you want for yourself and your family. You will have good assistance to maintain, improve, store, protect, and insure your assets so they grow in value and support you when you retire. You will have plans to protect loved ones from risks and arrange for the care of children, elderly parents, or pets in the event you are unable. If you own a business, your business legal, accounting, and financial plans will be in order. If you are married or have a life partner, good support from this network will engage both of you since these matters can be complicated and impact the surviving partner. The tendency of widows to engage a new financial planner within a year of a husband's death is one indication that support of that type is uncommon for many people.

Coming of age as an adult is not an event; it is a process of taking on additional responsibilities, and it begins earlier than you may recognize. It can start in high school if you have a job and report your income to the IRS. It most certainly begins when you enter college or trade school. If you are a young person making that transition today—or the parent of one who is—it may not yet appear there are assets to manage, but there are.

My own situation and that of a friend in college is instructive. When I was in graduate school (in the dark ages before laptops), I protected my work in several ways. I had my dissertation typed on the innovation of its day: a WANG word processor, for example. It was the only one in my Big Ten college town and offered the safety of electronic storage. For an added layer of insurance, periodically I mailed an updated copy to my mom for safekeeping. I heard that things stored in the freezer did not burn, so I placed a copy there and carried a current copy everywhere I went in an army-surplus backpack that never left my side. Lots of people got a good laugh at me. That is, until a fellow graduate student lost two years of research data compiled from cross-cultural studies she conducted in Japan and Mexico. Her boyfriend thought it would be nice to have a fire burning in the fireplace when she got home, so he lit one before heading to the airport to greet her as she returned from a research trip. They pulled in the driveway to see the house burned to the ground. I can't recall if she ever finished her degree, but I do know nobody laughed at me after that.

We didn't have digital assets or a digital footprint of social media accounts back then, but today those may be far more substantial for a high school or college student than for their parents. Various websites and the storage services they offer contain artistic and musical creations that are like virtual scrapbooks. Second Life and World of Warcraft Avatars may have financial or intellectual property holdings. Estate law is only now beginning to grapple with these assets, which cannot be controlled by anyone other than the owner, even in the event of death or disability, unless special arrangements are made in advance. Young people may have other assets as well, including a credit card, an automobile, a computer, and a bank account. These may seem small compared to those of their parents, but regardless of size or value, having legal documents in place so others can manage them if necessary is important. By the time students enter college, they also need to assure parents are authorized to manage their medical affairs in the event of a hospitalization or serious injury by assigning a health care proxy, signing HIPAA forms, and creating a living will.

If you have come of age, whether you know it or not, you need a home and personal affairs network of people to support you, and each one must be skilled in their field. If you haven't yet built this network, you should consider doing so. You should also assure that others who might need to help you in the event of an accident, injury, or serious illness can get access to information to help them do that. The "business of you" is far too complicated for most people to master alone. It can be difficult to manage during the best of times and impossible to manage during a long-term illness. Mismanagement can create lasting problems. Consider bill paying and home maintenance, for example, with your many connections with credit card companies, a landlord or mortgage holder, utility companies, and yard work services. Consider estate planning, which is far more involved than when earlier generations of your family planned theirs. Consider retirement planning, since you are likely to have a life three decades longer than previous generations. Consider end-of-life planning, since medical technologies can prolong your life even longer still. Consider business ownership, which complicates these matters even more, as noted in this infographic from SEI.

You're surrounded by advisors

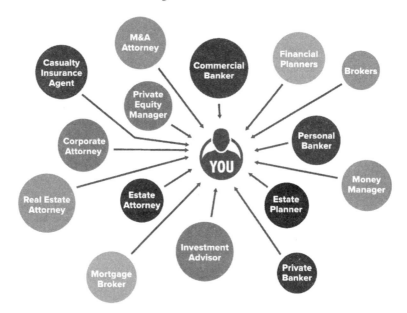

©2014 SEI

Matters pertaining to children are no less challenging. Though some laws are changing, most are based on traditional views of marriage and nuclear families, not same-sex marriage, divorce, and remarriage. Estate law and inheritance practices did not envision the reproductive technologies that allow children to be conceived after a parent dies. Child custody when parents divorce and child guardianship when parents die are not only emotionally charged but legally and financially complicated. Planning is difficult and not always adequate to protect children with special needs over the long term, as one client learned. "Our financial plan was to send our son to college, but then we found out that only 25 percent of kids like ours ever become independent of their parents. Our advisers never asked enough about our kids, and we didn't know to mention it. We caught it in time, but it was almost too late to build an alternative financial future."

Consider, as well, other ways in which advice can be correct but only partially so without the benefit of NetworkSage insights, as I eventually came to understand about home ownership. Buying a home was all about the numbers. The financial numbers, that is. The realtors, mortgage companies, financial planners, accountants, and the *New York Times* buy-rent calculator raised all the right financial questions. What is the home price-to-rent ratio? How long will you live there? Do you have job security? How much of a down payment can you make? What kind of mortgage would you like? A fixed rate? A variable rate? What will you spend on routine maintenance? Is the cost of renovations or a major project like a roof in your budget? Is the mortgage interest deduction tempting you to borrow more than is wise? What will this do to your debt-to-income ratio, especially if you're still paying off school loans, or if you plan to have a baby and take time out of the workforce? Will your real estate taxes skyrocket to support new schools in the area or cover municipal pension obligations? Is it worth the risk to put this many investment eggs in one basket?

Like many people in my generation and in that era, home owning was an American dream, and every adviser said it was a good investment decision. At some stages of my life, had I been aware of the rest of the numbers, my home buying decisions would have been different. What was missing? No one raised questions about whether I had the bandwidth to manage all the people required to maintain the home. I'm not surprised.

I've owned six different homes over forty-five years, but until I created my first pit crew list, I did not consciously appreciate the scope of the management demands property requires, especially during renovations. In retrospect, I am amazed I could ride herd on such a large group of workers and not be aware of the toll it took on me and other networks, especially those related to my career.

My first list also showed me how even just one of the people in my home-management network could "make or break" home owning. Two of my own experiences are instructive. In the first, faulty electrical wiring installation in new construction nearly caused a serious and deadly house fire in my townhome. It was discovered late one night with only hours to spare when I detected a strange smell and called on a neighbor to help investigate. It threatened not only my home but the homes of four other families. In the second, one Saturday afternoon, loud firecracker-like sounds came from the direction of a neighbor's yard when their tree split in half and came down on my roof. They'd not engaged a tree service, but I had a longstanding relationship with a good one that checked all my trees each year and removed or trimmed any that threatened my house. It never occurred to me to look across the property line to imagine a neighbor's tree could be a threat until it was too late. Happily, my good relationship with the arborist helped; he arrived within twenty minutes and removed the tree without any additional damage.

Inside This Network

I organize this network into five groups related to your primary residence, vacation home, investment properties, personal valuables, and personal affairs.

1. Primary Residence

What about you? Do you rent or own? If you rent, the number of people you manage to maintain your household is small. As a tenant, property management is not your responsibility unless you choose to take it on. That said, there are exceptions to this rule. Some landlords reduce rent if tenants cut the grass, for example. About one-third of renters live in single-family homes, and if you are one of them, you may maintain the exterior even in the absence of any rent reduction because you don't want your home to be a target for burglaries, you enjoy the exercise, or your children play there. Perhaps you plant gardens because you like homegrown tomatoes or enjoy entertaining friends in the outdoor spaces. These things are optional though. There's no contractual obligation to do it unless it's part of your rental agreement.

As a tenant, interior repairs are not your responsibility either, nor is maintenance beyond keeping the property free of public health and safety risks. You may be allowed to paint the interior, but there is no requirement you must do so, nor is there any economic incentive to make the effort. If the refrigerator stops working, it's not yours. You won't need to maintain a list of repair companies or pay for their work. Instead, you have just one point of contact to call: the landlord or property manager.

Once you own property, however, the number of people you need to support you grows quickly. As a condominium or co-op owner, you have full responsibility for the interior of your unit. You'll need utility companies, appliance maintenance and repair experts, a plumber, carpenter, painter, carpet cleaner, and chimney sweep if you have a fireplace. If you renovate, you'll learn as I did that the list will expand to include architects, designers, and contractors. In addition, because homeowner association, condominium, and co-op bylaws protect the collective interest of all the owners to maintain the value of the property, each renovation may require not only city health and safety inspector approval but also approval by the building's governing board.

Depending on the condominium or co-op property, you may have responsibility for the exterior. The building's management may provide some assistance, hiring contractors to tend to common grassy areas or wash the exterior windows, for example, but you will need to tend to any garden spaces you've planted. You may also have responsibility for spaces exterior to your unit but interior to the building as a whole—like the hallway outside your door. You might want plants or umbrella stands at your doorway, but building policies can prohibit items in the common hallways. In that case, it will be your responsibility to keep the hallway clear and to manage guests who arrive with strollers or on bikes.

If you own a single-family home, you become responsible for both the interior and exterior of the property and will need the largest support group of all. For the interior, your list will be like those of co-op and condominium owners. For the exterior, you may also need gardeners, landscapers, masons, exterior painters, roofers, septic tank cleaners, a snow removal contractor, tree trimmer, window washer, grass cutter, and animal and pest control experts.

When you purchase property, you'll also have to plan for changes in the seasons. Even as an experienced homeowner, I didn't account for the effort it would take to rake leaves on my large front yard in my suburban Philly home. It took more than my weekend. It took a crew! Nor did I arrange for snowplowing for my very long driveway, though I lived in snowy parts of the country my entire life! My first winter in that home announced itself with the sounds of shoveling outside my window before dawn one morning. The previous owner's snow removal contractor was already at work because he didn't know she'd sold the property. He showed up, as he had every year, to help her out. Lucky me, I had help waiting in the wings that I didn't know about and hadn't planned!

If, like most Americans, you want to remain in your home as you age, you will need to assure it is safe and convenient. Increasing numbers of interior designers, architects, and contractors are being trained and certified to adapt homes for the benefit of seniors. You can also benefit by providing names of anyone who helps maintain your home to other family members or friends who might someday be called upon to help you manage, especially if you become suddenly unable to do that because of an illness, injury, or other crisis.

2. Vacation Home

If you have a vacation home, you already know what Kevin learned. You need a network of people to support it as if it were a primary residence. Since it is not your year-round residence, it may be difficult to get insurance, so help from those who do preventive maintenance will be important to protect its value. You need others too, like someone who lives in the area year-round to watch over the property during the off season, especially to ensure that heating and cooling systems are in working order or to notify you of any storm damage or vandalism.

3. Investment Property

If you rent your vacation home to others or have other investment property, you need support as if it was your personal residence and more. You also need painting or cleaning crews between tenants and should pay utilities yourself to ensure no liens are placed against the property if tenants fail to do so. In addition, you may need rental agents and may have local municipality inspectors or licensing agencies to manage. You will need legal advisers to structure the rental arrangements and manage disputes that might arise with tenants. If your tenants fail to pay the rent and you pursue eviction in court, you may need help from an attorney and local sheriff. If disaster strikes any one of your properties, it is more complicated still. If you create a partnership with others, as Kevin considered, you need legal counsel to protect you from liability and accountants to ensure that financial gains or losses from the venture are reported correctly.

4. Personal Valuables

Even if you never own a home, it is likely that you have other valuables and need help to maintain and protect them. Auto dealers and mechanics, marinas, and insurers may be among those you'll need if you own a car, motorcycle, truck, boat, or RV equipment. You may also have computers, stereos, exercise equipment, appliances, home furnishings, art and antiques, designer clothing, and watches that need regular maintenance, seasonal storage, and, in some cases, special care from experts to keep them in working order and maintain their value.

5. Personal Affairs

As an adult, you need experts who provide you with legal and financial services, including bankers, insurance agents, accountants, attorneys, estate planners, and financial advisers. These individuals help you manage the risks of poor health, accidents and injuries, disability, property theft, disasters, and death. They insure your life, health, home, vehicles, personal property, and assets. They help create your financial plan and make investment decisions. They help you write a last will, make living will declarations, and establish powers of attorney. You also need friends or family who can be executors of your will, trustees if you have a trust, and, importantly, those who can act as your health proxy, advocating for your health care wishes if you are unable to do that yourself.

If you have children, pets, or act as a guardian for another person, you need the help of someone you trust to assume guardianship in the event of your death or disability, as well as skilled attorneys and financial planners to create the appropriate legal documents and develop solid financial plans to protect your love ones' futures.

Exploring Your Network

Recall your home growing up and how your parents managed it. Consider the degree of support they had from others, how that impacted their careers and lifestyle, and how that compares to your career, lifestyle, and household management needs today.

If you are considering a home or a vacation home purchase, determine all services you will need to maintain or improve it. If this is in a new area and you do not have existing connections with those who can help, determine if your seller, real estate agent, neighbors, or local friends can suggest reliable support services to engage.

Consider which legal documents would be necessary for a spouse, family member, friend, business partner, or adviser to use in the event someone needed to help manage your affairs. Assure they are current, organized, and stored in an accessible place. If you are responsible for the care of others—a child, elderly parent, ward, or pet—arrange for legal guardianship and financial plans to care for them in the event you are unable to do so.

If you are a senior with plans to live independently, determine whether renovations may be required to help you live there safely and to accommodate any special needs you have—or might have—in the future.

Key Points

- This network supports your need to manage, protect, and grow your property and other assets, including digital assets.
- It is the source of expert advice concerning your legal and financial affairs, providing you with the peace of mind that you and loved ones are protected.
- Coming of age is a process, not an event, beginning earlier than most people believe.
- It is wise to provide important contact information to another person, or keep it in a place they can find it, so they can help if the need arises.

Chapter 11

Ghost Networks

Invisible Support

TED AND JUNE MET in small-town high school and married right after graduation. The marriage did not last, and years later, Ted married again and with his new wife relocated to a city a three-hour drive away. June never remarried. She quit her job to care for her ailing parents and, when they passed away, lived with a twin sister and her family. Over the years, June reached out to talk with Ted as an old friend. Then, in her sixties, she was hospitalized with late-stage cancer. She knew chemotherapy was going to be a tough road and reached out to Ted for support. He gave it gladly, and his wife agreed it was the right thing to do.

Ted learned June had been hospitalized and arranged a trip to visit her. As they talked, he learned her cancer was far more serious than the original diagnosis indicated; treatments would not be effective, and she would not recover. It was then that Ted understood how strong old connections could be. He had once loved June, and they had remained good friends. He felt grief at the thought of losing her.

On the long drive home after the visit, he decided he needed to make the trip again the next day to see June once more. At first, he thought it would be difficult to tell his wife. Then he remembered they shared a common language about networks and the connections they had with others: people never really go away; they remain in your networks forever.

For Ted, June was a forever part of his family network. It didn't matter that he and June had divorced decades ago. It didn't matter that they didn't have kids to bind them. They were connected in an enduring former family, and that was all that mattered. Sticking with June during her final days was the right thing to do. When he arrived home that night and told his wife that June was part of his family network, she understood and supported his decision to return to see her.

Making the trip the next day with his wife's blessing meant a lot to Ted. To honor June's connection to his family and remembering how much his father had cared for June, Ted gave June one of his father's religious medals. They quietly talked, and he stayed until she fell asleep. Back at home the next morning, Ted got word that June had died during the night.

June's ashes were buried with his father's medal resting on top, and the following spring, Ted and his wife attended a picnic celebration to honor June's life. That was when Ted learned the rest of their story. June had remained connected to Ted's family network long after their divorce in a way he'd not known. On her own, quietly and without fanfare for more than forty years, June had tended Ted's parents' graves. During visits to his hometown, he'd visit the cemetery and notice how well they were tended. He always wondered who did it. Now he knows.

Network Role and Value

Yes, you read that right. Ghosts. They play a role in your life too.

Every person you encounter—whether a decades-long, intimate partner, a college roommate, a trusted teacher, a stranger you meet only briefly, or a pickpocket who steals your wallet—makes an impression on you. Our profoundly sophisticated brains take it all in, and neuroscience is only now beginning to understand how and how much. Evolutionary psychologists suggest this is one way we help ensure our own survival as we use the lessons learned in each encounter. Therein is the value ghosts have in the important lessons they taught us.

I didn't set out to find these long-lost connections when I started exploring networks, but they appeared in my own and others' experiences as we listed the people in our lives. As we shared stories, the importance of this network became clear. Regardless of how dear or influential people are or how long they are part of your life, in most cases, they do not remain with you forever. People pass away, move away, or drift away as life changes.

In fact, most of the people who were once very important to you are probably no longer present in your life. Consider the older generations of your family, elementary school best friends, pediatricians, high school confidants, and college roommates. Add to that list your favorite babysitters, piano teachers, coaches, and teammates. In your career, you've left colleagues behind as you changed jobs, got transferred, or earned promotions. In fact, especially if you got promoted, colleagues who were once an important part of your life may no longer be. If you were raised in a military family, you probably said goodbye to more people by the time you were eighteen than most of us will in a lifetime.

Calling them "ghosts" is a way to organize memories and recognize that, although these people are no longer physically present, you remain connected. I place ghosts within the bigger category of coming-of-age networks for a reason. You've been collecting them all your life as you moved, changed schools, changed jobs, left others behind, or were left behind by them. It's usually not until later in life, though, that the role they played is something you want to explore. Doing so is empowering in two ways. First, you can learn from the lessons they taught you when they were part of your life. Second, they can remind you that anyone in your life today may become a ghost later. Managing your connections with those things in mind makes life better for everyone, now and in the future.

Remembering Ghosts

Some ghost memories surface readily, and you'll be easily and consciously aware of who they were and what influence they had. As was the case for Ted, this can happen during times of great emotion and not only the emotions of loss or grief but also those of joy and exhilaration. Memories can also surface when you enter a new stage of life. Watching your children grow, for example, will remind you of your own childhood and people you forgot long ago.

Memories can surface when you go in search of them. Holidays are one of those times. As I write this, it is Thanksgiving week, a time of year when we recall others with gratitude. Memories can also surface when a coach or workshop leader suggests you identify people who influenced you. They can surface when you face problems, seek counsel from a therapist, and search for encounters that haunt you and rob you of peace.

Some memories will come to mind easily because you were connected to people for many years: those in your family, your school, your scout troop, army unit, or your religious congregation, for example. You will recall others because they were particularly influential, like the special friends, bosses, or mentors who shaped your career. You may have photographs and other reminders to help: old report cards or transcripts, recommendation letters, news articles, or legal documents, for example. Even one single, dramatic, kind event can trigger memories, like the kindness of a stranger who helped you change a flat tire on a rainy day. It would also be easy to recall traumatic events, like being mugged when you traveled in a strange city.

On the other hand, some memories will not surface easily or may reside only in your unconscious memory, perhaps buried forever. Both conscious and unconscious memories are important and play a role in how you react to people and situations. Mental health experts say that unconscious memories, especially, play a role in our inexplicable reactions—and especially overreactions—to people and events.

You Are a Ghost Too

Just as we have memories of others, they have memories of us as well, and it is worth recognizing that we may never know the impact of even our smallest contacts with them. In my case, a young career professional sought me out to thank me for a lunch we shared when he interned in my office during pharmacy school decades earlier. It was a powerful, humbling experience since I could not even recall the encounter, though he rated it as one of the top three positive influences in his career. That was an important lesson for me about taking care when connecting with others, especially those who were younger and in their formative years.

In her book, *Invisible Acts of Power: The Divine Energy of a Giving Heart*, medical intuitive, author, and speaker Carolyn Myss shares an even more subtle, powerful, and consequential example. She describes a young man who, on his walk home from work one evening, noticed a woman stopped at a traffic light. She noticed him as well, and although they did not know each other, she smiled at him. That was all, just smiled. In that moment, the young man changed the plans he'd made to end his life that night. It's likely that the woman herself never knew how profoundly transformative one smile could be. It's clear that the young man did.

Inside Ghost Networks

I organize this network into four groups: friendly ghosts, hungry ghosts, other ghosts, and role models.

1. Friendly Ghosts

These are the people who were helpful, loving, generous influences in your life. Perhaps, like me, you had a wonderful grandfather. Mine taught me generosity and the never-ending abundance of love. Though he passed away when I was quite young, I can still remember how wonderful it was to sit in his lap and how excited I'd be when he came to visit. He is imprinted in my memory forever, and in that way, he never really left me.

Perhaps your grandfather took you fishing or read you stories. Maybe you had a teacher, a coach, or a neighbor who cared for you in a special way. Perhaps a good physician or a wise clergyman inspired you to pursue your career, or a mentor arranged an introduction that got you promoted. You may even have a long-gone, beloved pet from your childhood who was there when you needed to confide in someone. If your family was not supportive, perhaps someone in your neighborhood or scout troop is now a friendly ghost because they stepped in, encouraging you to stay in school or helping you stay out of trouble.

Memories of friendly ghosts are worth retrieving. They lift your spirits and inspire you. There are probably days you wish you could thank them for all the wonderful ways they helped you, and you might wish they could see you now. These are the ones to remember when times are tough. For me, even a momentary thought about my grandfather reminds me that love is not a zero-sum game but a reality to be shared abundantly. In that way, the investment of love he made in me is still paying dividends more than a half century after his death.

2. Hungry Ghosts

These ghosts are the people who left a hole in your heart and wounds to heal. One summer intern told me about her grandmother, who at seventy-six years old has a ghost from first grade. Her teacher said she was not creative. Seventy years have passed since then, and she still refuses to attempt any "creative" endeavor. Imagine the tragedy.

I call these ghosts "hungry" because you could not satisfy them during the time you had together, and you can't satisfy them now either. You'll get no do-over with them, although mental health experts say you might still be trying—not with them in a literal sense, of course, but with people or in situations that remind you of them and trigger reactions.

The people in this network may have blamed you for their disappointments, failures, or unhappiness. They may have held you back, crushed your confidence, smashed your dreams, or broken your heart. They may have used guilt to manipulate you, called you names, bullied you, or told you outright that you were worthless. They may be thieves who stole your money, your optimism, your prom date, and your confidence in humanity.

You may have a hungry ghost in the teacher who shamed you because you forgot your homework or accused you of cheating on a test. Your hungry ghost may be the coach who said you weren't "man enough" for the sport. Perhaps you have an entire group of hungry ghosts in a middle-school clique that excluded you because you lacked the latest gear or couldn't afford the newest fashions. If lovers left, blaming you for the failed relationship, or colleagues stole credit for your work, they may be among the hungry ghosts that poke you into harmful overreactions to stressful circumstances. The wounds they leave behind can create lasting vulnerability.

Unfortunately, for many people, hungry ghosts show up at the most inopportune moments. I found hungry ghosts in all my networks, and they created mischief and sabotaged projects until I explored their influence. Though initially difficult, it was liberating. Now, on bad days when they show up in force, pitch a tent in my office, and taunt me, they are far easier to banish. The hard work of bringing them into awareness and putting them on a list robbed them of their power.

I'm not the only one who feels taunted, and the workplace is not the only place hungry ghosts appear. In the words of one executive whose situation was not resolved as well as Ted's was with June, "When we were married, I was very close to my wife's family, especially her two brothers. When we got divorced, she wouldn't allow them to see me, so I lost them. I travel for my job and didn't have many friends in town, so her brothers were a very important part of my social life. All the couples we knew stayed with her, and I lost them too. It was hard, and I thought the pain was over, especially since I got transferred and live in a new town. Then I heard she had cancer. I feel sorry for her, but her illness raised all the old pain, and this is not a good time. I'm engaged, and the wedding day is fast approaching. Now I have all these mixed-up feelings to deal with."

3. Other Ghosts

Once people started exploring ghosts, other categories emerged that did not quite fit the friendly or hungry ghost group, so I include this one as a separate group to encourage you to learn if there are other types of ghosts in your life. One teacher, for example, developed a "worry ghost" list for children who were no longer her students but whom she worried about nonetheless, either because of their learning problems or family situations. To balance that list, she also created a "happy ghost" list for students who had brightened her day. One young man created a "pet ghost" list, saying they didn't belong in any other category in his view. Other people thought that, though they were not connections in the way I've defined them here, the games they played as children had influenced them and deserved a way to be remembered, so they added those games to their ghost network.

4. Role Models

Once ghosts started showing up in networks, so did role models. These are people who were never a real, physical presence in your life but who were influential in some special way. They deserve a place in your networks too because they modeled values, lifestyles, behaviors, and success that you admire and find inspirational.

Some role models might be real historical figures from eras past.

You may admire Abraham Lincoln for all he accomplished despite his life's hardships, early political failures, and crushing depression. Others might be your contemporaries. Baby boomers like me might include Martin Luther King Jr. or John Kennedy, inspired by their life examples and accomplishments. Though she's not part of my generation, I admire Lady Gaga's courage and creativity. Now that she's singing with Tony Bennett, I admire her versatility as well.

Some of your role models might even be fictional characters. You might want to emulate the cool-headed, unflappable wisdom of Yoda from *Star Wars*, the adventuresome spirit of Tom Sawyer, or the storytelling skill of Anne of Green Gables. Maybe you're like me and admire Superman for how he bravely helped humankind all while disguising his identity and never seeking riches or fame, or *Iron Man* for the way he melds technology with a charming smile and a big heart. Did I mention I like superheroes?

Exploring Your Network

Thinking about each network is a way to recall ghosts, and it will be impossible to list them all because by the time you come of age, there are many. Of those that come to mind easily, take note of those who were loving and supportive, the ones I call friendly ghosts. What earned them a place on this list? Was it something they did? Or said? Then turn your attention to those I call hungry ghosts and do likewise.

List role models, especially those you recall from childhood, and identify any of their superhero qualities that rubbed off on you.

Consider how friendly ghosts support you today, how hungry ghosts sabotage you, and how role models inspire you. On a bad day, which ones exert the greatest influence?

Some people create additional ghost categories. Consider other ghost categories you could create.

Key Points

- Most of the people who were once important in your life may no longer be present.
- Even brief and superficial encounters can leave a lasting impact.
- Later in life is a time most people explore the impact of ghosts in their lives.
- Inexplicably strong reactions to people and events can signal the presence of forgotten ghosts.

Part 3

How to ACTSage

UNLIKE DRIVERS ON AN Indy 500 track, you need a road map. ACTSage is the traveler's guide to the NetworkSage road map. In step 1, using the *network information architecture* I described in part 2 of this book, you become *aware* of your network connections by making a list and displaying them as a list, an organization chart, or a mind map. In step 2, with the information in the *awareness* step and suggestions for contemplating your life and circumstances, you gain *clarity* about what you want or need from your network connections. In step 3, using the information from the *clarity* step, you make changes to *transform* your life.

As you begin these steps, it may be helpful to remind yourself about what you've read so far: that high-quality connections with real people you can see, feel, and touch are vitally important, and there are plenty of opportunities to do that within your eight networks.

That support is critically important because you are not a machine that can be refueled in a twelve-second pit stop in a race that will last only hours. You are a human being, sometimes traveling unknown territory, on roads with detours and potholes, and often without clear direction. It helps to have support to ensure that your body, heart, and mind remain engaged throughout the journey as you navigate.

Connections with others provide that support. Connections matter. They really do matter.

Build networks of people who support your dreams, and they will free up any pent-up potential to achieve them. You will be more likely to have good health, get a good education for your children, build your career, enjoy your retirement, and support the causes you care about. You will feel more settled and in control. You will have greater satisfaction and peace of mind.

Chances are your connections are helping you do that, and in turn, you are supporting others as they reach for their dreams. It's also likely that the converse is true and that you are connected to people who lack the skills to support you, don't share your values, or are unable to assist because they are overloaded. You may be connected to others you can't support well, perhaps for those same reasons.

Knowing that and understanding what to do about it is important for everyone, but it is especially important if you have big dreams, big responsibilities, or a big heart. It is vital if you're already overloaded— or might be in the future—as you chart your next career move, launch a business, start a family, face a crisis, or care for a seriously ill, disabled, or elderly family member. These chapters will get you started.

Chapter 12
ACTSage Step 1: Awareness

Laura's Big Reveal

LAURA WAS A WORKING mother. By the time we met, she'd already had successful careers in top companies known for their blend of innovative science and creative marketing. She had just stepped off the fast track to the presidency of a New York Madison Avenue firm to start her own firm. She was already fully booked with a portfolio of global company clients.

She was one of the most energetic people I've ever known and had the fighting spirit she needed to face a big challenge at home. She and her husband had two adopted sons; both had special needs. Laura never met a problem she could not solve. These were not going to be the exception. She attended seminars for families whose children had been diagnosed with Asperger's syndrome or ADHD, learned the ropes from other parents, and hired specialists. As a skilled, fearless advocate for her children, she was a formidable force on their behalf.

Nonetheless, over time, her efforts to manage their needs were starting to take a toll on her family life and new business. In 2010, three years into my own exploration of networks, I suggested she might want to give it a try. She was game. Listing the people in her networks was revealing, and when she finished, she declared it worth the effort.

"You liberated me. You gave me data. Now I have insights about my networks, how they work and where they don't. That's what I needed to start making changes."

The data? At the time, Laura was managing forty-seven people for just one of her sons, a then thirteen-year-old with Asperger's. Until she made network lists, she had not been aware. In a few short months, she was well under way making changes. In all, she reduced the number of people to eight by transferring him to a special school and making changes to a variety of other services he received. Her son was under the care of three female psychiatrists, for example. "He's thirteen now, and I want him to see a man," she told me, "and we found one who is good. But he's four hundred dollars an hour! I struggled with this for weeks, wondering if we could afford him. Now, I see the decision differently. I can fire the three women, hire the man, and come out ahead." She lowered the family's expenses, nearly eliminated the number of crises interventions that required her management skills, returned to her new business, and redirected her energy to other personal and family interests.

As I write this, it is six years later. Her son graduated from high school one year early, is in college, has a part-time job, and lives in an apartment with other young men. His younger brother has graduated from high school, been admitted to his preferred college, and Laura and her husband will soon be empty nesters. She called last week to say they were relocating to another state and used NetworkSage principles to guide them as they picked the realtor to help.

Hiding in Plain Sight

In the first ACTSage step, you will develop an awareness of the connections in your networks. Laura's experience and my own hint at the value of doing that. A study done on Harvard University students shows how challenging it can be.

The study was conducted by researcher, speaker, and author of *Beyond*

Happiness, Shawn Achor. He gave students three minutes to draw a map of Harvard Yard and Harvard Square, the territory where they lived, studied, and socialized, from memory. Objectively, the territory was the same for everyone, and maps are readily available. In fact, students had access to maps long before they arrived on campus and probably studied them to prepare for their first days of school. Yet, when asked, students' drawings did not match the objective versions. Instead, drawings represented students' subjective experiences, the ones that matched the life they lived, a map of their own design.

They put their favorite place in the center. In some cases, this was their dorm because they liked being there with friends. In other cases, it was a pub for similar reasons. They also adjusted the size of the buildings. Less studious students made the library a very small building or omitted it altogether. Most ignored nonstudent housing bordering the campus. Shawn Achor's study addressed the degree to which students were aware of their physical environment, and the results showed that their awareness was distorted and did not match objective reality.

We have a similar experience where our connections are concerned. We focus on people most important to us or those we must attend to immediately, as did Laura when she intervened to help her son at school. Under nearly constant stress, until Laura made a list, she didn't appreciate the number of connections she was managing—and often, paying—on her son's behalf. She focused only on the smaller number involved in the educational or health crisis of the moment.

I can understand why. After all, I wasn't under stress at the time I created my list, but nonetheless, I failed to include my accountant and forgot the guy who plowed my driveway. It wasn't tax season or winter, so they were not top of mind. Like those Harvard students and their subjective maps of the campus, Laura and I failed to see our networks objectively, accurately, or comprehensively. Like students ignoring nonstudent housing, we ignored some connections. They may have been in plain sight, but to us they were hidden.

That is why I created the *network information architecture* described in part 2 to help you find your connections, especially any that may be hiding just outside your immediate, conscious awareness because you did not see or need them today, or even, in this very moment. Especially during this first ACTSage step, if you refer to those chapters as you become aware of your connections, it will be faster and far more accurate and complete for you than it was for me when I began. This chapter will give some ideas about how to do that.

Make a List

The simplest way to answer the "Who are the people in my networks?" question in this first, ACTSage, *awareness* step, is to make a list, just like the first pit crew list that I did. As you do, I have some tips to help make it faster, easier, and more accurate.

Don't Aim for Perfection

A list need not be perfect. It only needs to be good enough for how you intend to use it. For example, if you're creating a list only to learn the size of your networks or to take a big-picture look at all your responsibilities and connections, it's not necessary to use each person's full name. For most connections, it will be good enough to use just their first name or the service they provide you. For example, it can be good enough to list them as Aunt Jane or as doctor, dentist, roofer, or landscaper.

As I will mention later and explain why, eventually you will want to add full names and contact information, but don't do it at the beginning. If you interrupt list making to recall full names, or search your contact database to spell names correctly or add contact details, you'll lose momentum, become frustrated, and quit before you've finished.

You First

Since you are your most important *primary connection*, create your list first and cover all your bases. When you are satisfied with your own list, turn to your other primary connections, like children, pets, elderly parents, or business teams and create lists of connections who help you with your responsibilities to the important people in your life. Here is an example: if you have children, they are in your family network, in a group I call "your family today." When you are satisfied that your own network list is good enough, near the name of each child, list the connections in the child's five birthright networks near their name. Include such people as physicians, teachers, coaches, and parents of your children's friends. If you have elderly parents, they are also part of your family network, in a group I call "your family of origin." Near their names, you can list the names of their physicians, friends, neighbors, and handyman, especially if you already—or someday need to—interact with them to help your parents.

If you have more than one child, even if the same pediatrician cares for all your children, that physician is a separate connection you manage for each child and should be listed separately by each child's name. That is because each child may react differently to the pediatrician, kids rarely get sick or need care at the same time, and well-child visits are scheduled based on each child's age, not for your convenience of getting care for all your children at the same visit. Since most physicians now practice in a group, it is important to note all of those who might provide care for your child and to make a special note if you or your child has a favorite.

As an easier alternative, rather than include all these connections near their names on your own list, use a separate piece of paper for each child and list all their connections on that page. If you do that, however, it's important to remember that although the list is on a separate page, these are connections you manage as part of your parenting responsibilities. Creating lists for pets, elderly parents, work teams, or community volunteer groups dependent on you is a similar process.

Avoid Overthinking

As you use the network information architecture to recall people and add them to your list, it will be obvious that I have placed some people within one network when they may, in fact, be properly placed in several different ones. For example, does your weekly tennis group or walking club belong in the *health and vitality network* or in the *social and community network*? Should yoga or long mountain hikes you do with friends be included in the *spiritual network* or in the *health and vitality network* or in the *social and community network*?

Decisions like those are yours to make, based on the reasons you have chosen to add those people to your networks. If you hike with friends for social reasons, their names belong in your social and community network. If you hike as part of fitness goals, they belong in your health and vitality network. If you hike for both reasons, their names belong in both networks for reasons that will become clear when I discuss ways to use the connection information you collect at this step. The network information architecture is intended to be flexible and to serve you, so use it as you like and don't feel constrained by my way of organizing or defining connections. For example, even though my dad has been deceased for more than two decades, his name remains within my family network. I have not moved him to the ghost category because he remains "present" in my life.

Remember that at this stage you are creating awareness, so avoid overthinking where you might eventually place each name on the list. It's more important to remember the people you want to include and list them somewhere—or everywhere—to keep the momentum going so that you finish and have a "good enough" list for the next ACTSage step.

Expect "Network Crush"

Expect a feeling I call "network crush." That's a feeling very much like overwhelm. You may have felt something like it when you cleaned out a garage, did your taxes, or cleared the top of your desk. It happens to everyone when they work on their list. It happened to me, and I had a relatively simple life!

Becoming *aware* of all your connections as you make a list is not difficult intellectual work, but it can be emotional. You may be surprised—even dismayed—to see the large number of connections you manage on an ongoing basis. Your heart may ache as you are reminded of those you love but don't see often enough. You may feel angry as you see some support connections are taking your good nature for granted and not providing quality services. You may feel frustrated you can't break connections with in-laws, neighbors, or colleagues who create stress. You may also feel regret or guilt when you're reminded of those you've disappointed.

When "crush" happens, go easy on yourself. Give yourself credit for getting started! Take a break, a deep breath, and relax. Laura took a break for a glass of wine midway through. Then, remember what organizing experts say about the value of cleaning out and clearing clutter: peace of mind. You feel more confident, in control, and at ease when you're organized. You will soon feel that same way about your networks. Remember, too, what Laura said: "You liberated me. You gave me data."

Include All Networks

Network crush may tempt you to focus on some of your networks and ignore others. Please resist the temptation and try to identify connections from all eight on your list. The benefits from including most of your connections in all eight networks will be far greater than if one or two networks are complete at the expense of ignoring the rest. The reason for this will be clear when you read about the next ACTSage steps in chapters 14 and 15, but here are some hints about why. Sometimes a problem in one network originates in another. Other times, a solution to a problem in one network can be found in another. Ignoring a network will deprive you of those insights.

Refine Lists Later

Having complete names and contact information for everyone on your list is critically important when others help you manage your affairs, and that happens to all of us eventually. For those reasons, though it is a tedious project, it is something you will want to do eventually. This is far more important than most people appreciate.

Just as many of your connections are hiding in plain sight, the complexity of your life is too. Adult lives do not become complicated overnight. As we come of age, we add responsibilities and connections gradually, incorporating information about each one into our personal—and sometimes idiosyncratic—management systems. These help us be efficient and responsible and may be "good enough" for our own use. None of us knows the future, however, and when we might need help from others. In times of crises, even if our systems are well organized, they can be impossible for another person to access or difficult to use unless we organize with that in mind.

I watched a friend realize this over dinner one night. He was a NetworkSage for his business but could not understand the value in any other part of his life. That night, as he told me his daughter and new son-in-law were on a flight returning from their honeymoon, it finally dawned on him. He said, "If that plane crashed, it would not be easy for me to step in to help. I have only one phone number for her at work and one for a friend. I don't even know where they boarded the dogs."

That situation applies to most people. If you are single, a sudden illness or injury will require help from others to manage your affairs during your recovery. If you have a spouse or life partner, is it likely you have divided the workload; one of you has information about children's schedules, household help, or finances that the other does not. If you are an older person, your adult children or a close friend may need to contact your physicians, household help, neighbors, or attorney, not only in the event of an emergency but perhaps to help you live independently.

Refining your lists by adding contact information will give you peace of mind. Sharing the lists with those who need to know—or telling them where to find the information—will help reduce the impact of disruptions if any occur. In several families I know, the unexpected death of young wives and mothers left husbands without such basic information as the name of their children's pediatrician and dates of upcoming school events. In another, the untimely death of a husband left his wife without contact information for the attorney he engaged to revise their last will to add their most recently born child, or business ventures that supported the family's income. In another case, the sudden death of a thirty-year-old, single man at his office one afternoon left his fiancée and parents without information to help settle his affairs. It took them two years to do so. A widow I know has been unable to discontinue her husband's cell phone service; she did not know his password or the answer to security questions like the name of his favorite restaurant in college or third-grade best friend. In today's complicated world, with its entrepreneurial and small-business economy, geographic mobility, and distant family members, it is more important than ever that contact information for your important connections be assembled and available.

Avoid Existing Databases

It can be tempting to believe a database like Microsoft Outlook Contacts, Facebook, or LinkedIn might be a helpful reference guide as you create a list.

They can be helpful for verifying information and adding contact information later but not for generating your list. Why? These databases can be very large, with many entries archived for your convenience. They are not relevant to your most important, ongoing, network management needs, however. If you use them as a guide, it will take more time and effort to sort people "out" than if you use the network information architecture described in part 2 to recall and sort people "in." I know, because I've tried it.

In addition, those databases are flawed. How? They won't remind you that someone important might be missing. For example, it is unlikely you would be reminded of your physician or plumber by Facebook, or recall your dentist or attorney scanning LinkedIn connections. And if none of them are in your Outlook contacts or iPhone, neither will remind you to find one. My network information architecture will.

What's Next?

When you've completed your first list, even a quick glance will show you something new about your life: the size of your networks, the support you have available, and the gaps you need to fill to live it well. I know from experience that even a simple "good enough" list helps! It gave me useful information I didn't already have, and the big reveal was this: I was managing far too many people to do it well. Seeing 139 people on my list explained some of my fatigue and frustration. I never calculated the amount of time I spent managing each one; I didn't need to do that. The length of the list was enough information to show me I needed to make changes and where I might do that easily.

Everyone has a similar experience. Even at this early stage without any of the contemplations described in the second ACTSage clarity step, they have insights. Some see they cannot sustain their number of social connections and community responsibilities and still maintain their health. Some see ways to simplify family life. Others learn they are dependent on spouses for far more than they knew, not only for marital, childcare, household management, and financial welfare but also for IT and bookkeeping support for their business. Still others recognize that their retirement plans are flawed and their desire to relocate will disrupt connections with those who provide important support services.

Since I didn't have network categories at the time, I could not organize my list, but since my network categories are available now, you can create your list based on networks right from the start. If you do that, you'll be able to see not only the total size of all your networks but also the size of each one separately and how they compare.

One final reminder: don't forget about yourself. If you've not done so already, add your name to the list and make sure it is at the top.

Create an Organization Chart

Eventually, I looked for ways to organize my list and group names on it into meaningful categories that have since become the network information architecture. I also experimented with ways to visualize the data. Using the connections on my list, I created an organization chart like the one here.

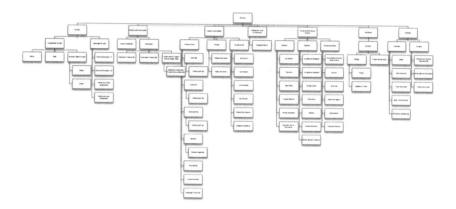

You are probably familiar with charts like these since they are often used in workplaces. I had access to software to help, but even if you don't, a display like an organization chart is easy to draw in your journal or on other paper, placing a name or connection type in each box. You can also create one using Post-it notes. Place a name or type of connection on each Post-it note and place each note on the wall or on a large piece of paper arrayed like an organization chart.

Creating an organization chart will help you gain an instant visual image of the size of each of your individual networks in a way that one long list cannot. It is also a fun family exercise. Children enjoy it, and it's a way to learn more about children's lives at school, in sports, and with friends.

If you already developed a list, you can use it to create a chart, but you don't need to develop a list first to successfully create a chart. You can begin with a chart by placing your name at the top and organizing lines and boxes for each of the networks below it. Then add people's names or roles, referring to my network information architecture.

I have some tips if you choose to develop a chart.

List-Making Tips Apply

Like lists, if you choose to develop a chart, don't aim for perfection. Make your chart good enough for the use you intend, adding contact details later. Create your own chart first; then add names or create separate charts for those in your care. As with list making, don't overthink, do expect to feel the overwhelm of network crush, avoid the temptation to focus only on some networks, and be as complete as you can for all eight. Use the network information architecture as your reference guide rather than Microsoft Outlook Contacts, Facebook, or LinkedIn.

Don't Be Misled

I have one additional, very important tip if you choose to create a chart. When you interpret the information, remember that organization charts were created to help us understand connections within one of our networks: our workplaces. They describe hierarchies and chain of command. Even in a small company and in today's collaborative work environments, everyone has a boss and must be responsive to that boss. Most people also have employees who, in turn, are responsive to them. Workplaces have rules about behavior, and there are consequences for breaking them. Step outside your workplace and there are different rules.

I learned this hierarchy lesson, but it took a long time. I posted the organization chart in my office and used it for nearly a year before another big reveal: I was not a company with multiple divisions. In my government and corporate jobs, where I had far greater responsibilities than in my personal life, I had no more than three direct reports. In my personal life, however, I had 139! That is far more personnel to manage than any employer would expect or any human resources professional would allow.

Worse yet, since workplace rules didn't apply, getting along and getting what I needed was harder. No wonder a hairdresser and physician felt they could keep me waiting and getting timely service from an accountant and attorney took not only a retainer but constant reminders and deadline renegotiations. That didn't happen in my work life. The organization chart I created for my personal-life networks gave me a false sense of control. No wonder I felt overloaded and underresourced. It wasn't only the size of my networks; the rules were different. I wasn't the boss.

Realizing I wasn't the boss wasn't a blow to my ego. Rather, it was a wake-up call to change my life, simplify my lifestyle, build better networks, and think about my connections differently. Despite decades of management experience, I had created a personal life that required I manage more people than was humanly possible. Having so many direct reports in my personal life wasn't sage.

Because organization charts were a misleading way to visualize my networks, I went looking for a better way, one that did not falsely imply I was the boss. That's when I found mind maps.

Draw a Mind Map

Mind mapping is a technique developed by British author and educational consultant Tony Buzan. I'm a fan of all his work, including mind maps. A mind map shows relationships among various pieces of a whole idea. It is a visual thinking tool that helps to better organize, analyze, and recall ideas. It is simple yet powerful. It is a picture that focuses on one idea, which is placed at the center and then surrounded by related elements. Mind maps are used for a variety of business and creative endeavors, and software packages to help draw mind maps are available. Even without those tools though, mind maps are easy to draw by hand, as you may recall from the story about Krissie and her extended family in chapter 4.

To create a mind map of your networks, place the one "idea" that is the focus of the drawing at the center of a page. In this case, at the start, that "idea" is you. After you have placed your name at the center, draw branches outward for each of your eight networks. Because each network has subgroups, any subgroup relevant to you then becomes a subbranch of its respective network, and the people in each of the subgroups are listed there. Post-it notes on a wall can be used to create mind maps just like they do to create an organization chart. If you have photographs of people, you can post those on a wall or very large piece of paper as well.

Each of the tips about how to create lists applies to mind maps as well. Like lists, if you choose to develop a mind map, don't aim for perfection. Your mind map must only be good enough for the use you intend, adding contact details later. Create your own mind map first; then add names or create separate mind maps for those in your care. Don't overthink, do expect to feel the overwhelm of network crush, avoid the temptation to focus only on some networks, and be as complete as you can in all eight. Use the network information architecture as your reference guide rather than Microsoft Outlook Contacts, Facebook, or LinkedIn.

Mind maps are an improvement over lists and organization charts, which is why they are my preferred way to display my own networks. Why? Unlike lists, mind maps are not linear. They are a more accurate reflection of the tapestry of our networks and connections. Unlike organization charts, mind maps do not create the false impression that personal networks are like workplaces with hierarchies that make management easier. Most of all, I like mind maps because, better than any other display, they remind you of another important NetworkSage principle: as connector-in-chief, you belong at the center of your networks, as I am in this mind map created from my initial list of connections.

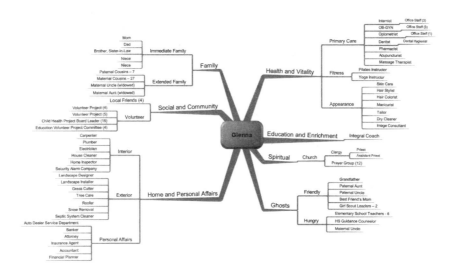

Whether you've chosen to develop lists, create an organization chart, or draw a mind map for the first time, you might see why creating work-life balance can be so challenging. Current approaches to achieving balance do not account for the number, size, and complexity of networks either inside or outside of our workplaces. You might also see why providing care for a child, a parent, or a pet can be so demanding and why it is important to share your network connection information with someone who might need to care for you.

Now that you have reached the end of this first *awareness* step, it is likely you have identified changes you want to make. Most people do.

If so, don't hesitate to make them now, especially if they are easy and doing that will help you to simplify your life and free up the time and energy you need to take the next steps. If not, don't worry. The next chapter will help. It will describe the second ACTSage step and show you additional ways to gain *clarity*.

Key Points

- Important connections are hiding in plain sight.
- A list, organization chart, or mind map can help you find and visualize connections.
- Aim for a good enough list and expect network crush.
- Include all networks and provide important contact information to another person, or keep it in a place they can find later.

Chapter 13

ACTSage Step 2: Clarity

THE FIRST ACTSAGE *AWARENESS* step was enough for me to know I needed to make changes and to get started doing it. It's that way for everyone. If your experience is like ours, you may already be clearing out some of the dysfunctional support or transactional connections that have been wearing you down. You may have set better boundaries and no longer tolerate poor service. You may be taking time to care for your health and well-being. You might already be making more money and have more free time. In the case of Carl, the attorney you met in chapter 9 when I described career networks, it took only two months to pare down the size of his client list, increase his income, and play more golf. He had more energy and felt better about life, and his wife was happier, which pleased him even more.

If you've already started to make changes like these, you're at the important tipping point in your journey as a NetworkSage. What you've done so far may have created enough improvement in your life, and you might be tempted to stop here. I encourage you, though, to take this second ACTSage clarity step, and for two reasons.

First, time and again I've seen how—just like when closets, garages, and desktops are cleaned—new opportunities arrive. It's said that nature abhors a vacuum, and perhaps that's why. If you've created space in your networks by clearing out unsupportive, stressful, or toxic connections, it's very likely that new people, projects, or ideas have arrived in your life, each one involving new connections. How will you decide which to pursue? Gaining clarity will help you choose more wisely.

Second, remember your potential? Remember the vast human capital at your disposal? Remember those dreams you left behind because you felt overloaded and the barriers seemed insurmountable? Are those still alive within? Is now the time to recommit to them? If so, remind yourself again that being connected to the right people can make the difference between success and failure. Your networks are your personal ecosystem, and, like environmental ecosystems, they need to be healthy to support you at all stages of life and in all the ventures you pursue. Clarity will help you ask the right questions, find the right answers, and assure good connections are there to support you as you take those important next steps.

Pathways to Clarity

There are four different paths you can take to gain clarity. You can travel just one or explore them all.

- Focus on networks.
- Focus on connections within networks.
- Focus on life events and risks.
- Focus on life plans.

Whichever you select, along the way you can enhance your list, organization chart, or mind map by keeping notes in your journal or on the worksheets downloaded from www.sagemylife. In addition, at this stage you can use colors or symbols to add at-a-glance power to any visual images you have created. It's easy to do. For example, some people use colored markers to highlight names. Green markers to indicate good helpful connections, like lifelong friends or a specialist physician who diagnosed a child's troubling symptoms. Yellow markers highlight acceptable but high-maintenance connections, like moody friends or contractors who show up on time but leave a mess to clean up. Red markers are used for stressful or toxic connections, like hypercritical relatives or schoolyard bullies.

Some people draw emoticons or buy emoticon sticker sheets to use in addition to colors. If you used Post-it notes to create network charts or mind maps with children, those have plenty of space for emoticon stickers. People use symbols like check marks, plus signs, and minus signs to gain clarity and point the way to changes they will make. One new mom used plus signs to remind her of those she could turn to for assistance and advice and minus signs for those she found critical of her parenting decisions. This at-a-glance view led her to join a Facebook parenting group to increase the number of helpful people and to learn better how to handle the critics from more experienced moms. One friend starting a new business placed a dollar sign by the name of each person who could help him be successful. Some place a gold star by the names of those who are a primary connection and a blue star by those who are support connections, leaving those who are transactional connections with no star at all to serve as a reminder of the distinctions they made about those three connection types. One dad created an organization chart, placed hearts and stars by his children's names, and showed it to them, telling them about the important place they had in his life, which led to a family discussion about how they could all support one another. One business woman enlarged her network mind map to poster size and posted it at home to study over a period of weeks. She told me it reminded her of a garden, one that needed to be tended carefully to assure that pulling weeds didn't damage favorite flowers. It helped her make a complicated set of decisions, and over the next several months, she changed her living situation, arranged for alternative senior care for her mother, tripled the footprint of her storefront business, and created a nonprofit to support women with cancer.

Network Clarity

Focusing on networks overall will show you a big-picture, top-down look at your life, much like the view from a helicopter as you hover over landscape below. This perspective can point you in the general direction of changes you may want or need to make. This was the one that helped me see that although my home and property were beautiful, they were also a time-consuming management burden. That insight catalyzed my decision to sell the property and relocate to a much smaller, lower-maintenance place.

The Big Picture

From the big-picture perspective, this is probably the first time you've seen your life this way. Through this lens, you can see if your networks, overall, are working for you. You can see the degree of harmony or discord and which networks are most aligned with the vision you have for the life you live and the work you do.

Some networks will stand out as providing you with better quality support than others, and from this perspective, you may understand why. You may see networks where you are most comfortable and feel you best fit and those in which you feel like an outsider or want to avoid. You may also see which networks are the easiest or most difficult to manage, or which will be easiest or most difficult to transform.

Birthright Networks

Your birthright networks created an enduring legacy for you that you may wish to explore. Consider, for example, the people your parents invited into those networks, the impact they had on you, and the degree to which they remain a part of your life today.

Recall how those networks changed as you became more independent and able to select your own friends and choose where you would live, what you would study, and how you would engage socially in your community.

If you are a parent today, think about the networks you are creating and managing for your children. Determine if any changes are needed to those networks to help you to better care for them and assure their health, safety, education, and development.

Whether for yourself or others in your care, make a note of what you need from these networks now to create the life you envision for the future. Make special note of any important connection missing from any of your—or a loved one's—birthright networks.

Coming-of-Age Networks

Think about the coming-of-age networks you created for yourself. Consider what coming-of-age networks your parents created for themselves, how those have influenced you and whether any can help you now.

Note how these networks changed to accommodate a new job, a new home, a new baby, relocation, or retirement. Consider likely changes you anticipate in the future and note what support you need from these networks to create the life you envision. Note if there are important connections missing from any these networks.

Network Overlap

Notice if connections appear in more than one network and determine if that is a strength or weakness overall. Especially if these people are important sources of support, if they were suddenly unavailable, would you or others in your care be vulnerable? Determine whether you should develop backup plans in the event you needed to call upon others for help.

Connection Clarity

Focusing on your connections will give you the ground-level view of the people in your networks. Like the big-picture view of networks, this perspective can point you in the direction of changes you may want or need to make, this time at the level of the individual people.

Individual Connections

Looking at the connection in each network, assess who is supporting you and who is not, who is high maintenance and who is low maintenance. Identify those who consistently give you wise—or unwise—advice or those who generously share—or withhold—the benefit of their experience.

Identify those who would be there to support you if you suffered a health crisis, a career setback, or a really bad day.

Assess whether those who provide you with services you need—for example, health care, financial planning, home repair, or childcare—deliver what you need at a price you feel is fair.

Determine if you or someone in your care has an unmet need because the right person is not yet in their—or your—networks. If so, determine if any of your existing connections can help find the right person to fill that gap.

Consider the network management demands of important people in your life—a spouse or life partner, parent, sibling, friend, boss, or employee—and contemplate how that might impact their ability to maintain a good connection with you.

Role Connections

Identify your primary connections. For each one, in just a few words each, list your intentions and identify the support connections already helping you meet them. In this exercise, be sure to begin with yourself. Identify the support connections helping you achieve your goals for your health, education, social life, spirituality, or career. Next, consider those in your care: your children, pets, elderly parents, or in-laws. Identify the support connections helping you address their needs.

Notice if you need new connections to help you achieve your intentions as a parent, caregiver, or community volunteer. If you do, identify those in your networks who can refer you to good support connections.

Determine if transactional connections are draining you of time and energy, and if so, decide how to make changes to ease the burden.

Trust Connections

In each network and especially in important areas of your life when you must rely on others, assess the degree to which you trust your connections. Consider who among your friends will keep a confidence, who will watch over your home when you travel, and whether physicians and legal and financial advisers are easily accessible and provide trustworthy advice. Consider whether you have staff and colleagues you can trust to perform their job responsibilities, and business advisers or vendors you trust to deliver value at a good price.

If you are responsible for the health and welfare of a child, a seriously ill spouse, or elderly parent, identify those you trust to help, especially when you are not there to supervise.

Disconnections

In each network, note whether you will disconnect from some people. Determine the implications not only for you and that person but for others you—and/or they—connect with.

If you plan to disconnect from any primary connections, determine if you need advice and counsel from professionals to assure your integrity and compassion and to avoid creating hungry ghosts.

Life Event Clarity

Two types of events happen in our lives: those we plan and those we don't. You may be facing a big life event, like a wedding. You might also face an event you didn't plan, like a job loss. Keeping networks in mind as you navigate can help.

Planned Events

If you are planning a major event, and especially one that will be the first time for you—a wedding, a child's college selection, or a relocation—assess the impact on your connections and networks.

Determine if you have the bandwidth to manage any additional connections you will need to your networks as you manage the event and whether you are connected to people who may have advice or can help you succeed.

Unplanned Events

Unplanned events happen to everyone. It's not a question of whether but when. When they happen, they can require tremendous time, energy, and skill to manage. Fortunately, with some imagination about what might happen and planning in advance, it is possible to mitigate any damages.

Determine if you have the network management bandwidth for a sudden, unplanned event. If you are already "maxed out" or overloaded, determine where you might be able to cut back if needed.

Focusing on each network, imagine an unplanned event that could occur and how you might manage if it did. If you are newly pregnant, for example, how might you manage if you found you were having triplets? If your company merged with another, how would you manage through the transition to keep your job, or use that opportunity to find a better one?

Risk Events

Within each of your networks, there may be common risks you can anticipate, prepare for, or perhaps prevent altogether.

In your family network, for example, determine if a genetic condition places you at risk and what appropriate steps you will take to prevent it or to prepare for any inevitable disability. In your career, determine if changes in your industry pose risks to your employability and whether additional training or career networking will prevent a job loss. If you live in a disaster-prone region, determine if you have an adequate evacuation plan—especially for young, old, or disabled family members and pets—and good connections with an insurance agent, plumbers, electricians, or others who can help repair damage.

Life Plan Clarity

Your life plan—even better, a written plan—increases the likelihood you will achieve it. Luck, it is said, favors the prepared, and this is one way to create luck. Keeping networks in mind as you plan can help. Consider Kevin, who you met in chapter 10, and his decision against creating a vacation mountain-house timeshare with friends. Thinking ahead and using his business acumen, he could envision financial and legal entanglement if the relationships soured. Did it deprive his family of enjoying time with the others? Not at all. As an alternative, they jointly rent mountain homes. Kevin's ability to plan with his entire life and networks in mind helped him see they did not need to create a timeshare business to enjoy family vacations together.

Mastermind Plans

Some people join a mastermind group, which is a small group of peers who share experiences and advise one another. In most cases, these groups help grow businesses and careers, but gathering with peers of any kind qualifies as a mastermind group in my view.

Consider whom you would invite to a group of peers that would support any part of your life—in your career, as a parent, family caregiver, engaged community leader, or active retiree. Explore your profession or community and determine if there is an already formed group you could join. Imagine what you would want from this group.

Superhero and Antihero Plans

Every network has a center of gravity that pulls you toward it. I like superheroes because they set the bar high, creating a higher center of gravity that pulls you in that direction. Friend up and spend more time with them to learn from their superpower.

Determine if there are antiheroes in your networks, creating a lower center of gravity that pulls you down and decide whether you need to make changes and limit your contacts, or even disconnect.

Daily Plans

As your day ends, review it through the lens of your networks. Assess the quality of interactions with your primary connections. Review how your support connections helped you. Notice if there were times you were distracted or drained by transactional connections.

Imagine tomorrow and the people in each of the networks you will engage. Are you prepared to do it well? Do you have the support you need? Determine how you will engage others to get the help if you need it. Determine whether there are energy-draining connections you want to avoid.

Annual Plans

If you routinely look back at the start of a new year to review the one before and plan for the one to come, in addition to focusing goals, events, and outcomes, focus on your networks.

Consider the quality of interactions with your primary connections and assess how your support connections helped you to realize the goals you set. Create a plan for the coming year, identifying those connections that can be helpful. Schedule a time to talk with them about what you will need.

Make a list of the appointments you need with important support connections—like physicians, attorneys, financial planners, and accountants, especially if you might postpone them until "someday." Note them on your calendar now.

Caregiving Plans

If you care for a loved one—or soon will—determine what support you will need from your networks to do it well and engage their support.

If you are the sole caregiver, identify connections who can provide backup support so you have some respite for care. Also, identify any who could provide care for an extended time if you were suddenly unavailable because of your own illness or injury.

If several people and/or agencies are assisting you in caregiving, determine if you can improve coordination or assign coordination tasks to someone else to make it easier or less time-consuming for you.

Big Dream Plans

List your big dreams for yourself, your children, your business, or your community. Determine who among your connections can help achieve them. Identify any who can provide wise counsel or a helping hand to accelerate your progress and assure success.

Identify those people you are helping to achieve their big dreams and do likewise; determine if there are ways to accelerate their progress and assure their success.

Key Points

- Gain greater clarity by focusing on your networks, connections, life events, risks, and plans.
- Create an at-a-glance enhancement of your list, organization chart, or mind map with colors and symbols meaningful to you.

- Assess the strength and readiness of your current connections to provide the support you need, including in the important roles you have supporting others.
- Identify connections that are missing and develop plans to add them.
- Determine if there are changes or disconnections from others that need to take place and develop plans to do that.

Chapter 14
ACTSage Step 3: Transformation

IF I HAD MY way, we'd each have a superhero at the ready for whenever we needed one. In truth, that's what we have in our networks. Having arrived at the third step of the NetworkSage journey, you are now more *aware* of everyone in your networks and have greater *clarity* about what you need from them. You may have started to make changes and already feel the effects *transformation* creates. If you are interested in going deeper into transformative possibilities and accelerating your progress even more, this is the chapter that will help you. It builds on the plans you created during the ACTSage clarity step.

Sometimes you can create a change without telling others or engaging their help. I didn't tell anyone I was turning off my phone to avoid late-night calls, for example. I just did it. Nor did I tell others I hired a student to help me run errands. Laura didn't announce that she was recovering from the near-daily crises caused by the school's handling of her son's special needs by getting some massages. She just did it. You don't need to announce that you will no longer accept leadership roles in volunteer groups. You can simply decline when you're asked. If you feel you're spending too much time on social media, you can cut back. If you want more face-to-face time with friends, you can invite them to coffee or out for a walk without announcing your intention to have a more connected social life.

Many transformational steps, however, will involve others. Sometimes this will be necessary as you search for and engage new connections to fill the holes in your networks. Other times this will happen as you terminate a connection with an unreliable service provider or a toxic friend. It may also happen because, with greater clarity, you set better ground rules about managing connections.

Laura is a good example of someone who changed the ground rules, which she did when she relocated her son to a new school. Another "reveal" for her, besides forty-seven people she managed for him, was that she was the "mediator-in-chief" on his behalf. For years, she had stepped in to settle disputes among teachers and school administrators at the public school. She informed educators at the new school, "There are eight of you. You are experts. If there is a problem you can't resolve together, pick one of you as a spokesperson to call me." She told me afterward, "Enough is enough. At his old school, I was the go-between, wrangling with teachers, principals, and counselors three times a week because they did not agree with one another about how to handle him. It's been a great turnaround. Now, they're working for me!"

Selecting Transformation Targets

There are several ways to select transformation targets. To make it easier, I have some tips to pass along from those of us who have done it.

Select Easy Targets

It is tempting to dive right in to transform networks or connections you find most problematic. A NetworkSage would caution against that. Here's why. If you've been overloaded and underresourced, reaching this step can lift your spirits. Just being aware of your networks and gaining clarity can give you an exhilarating boost of energy even before you take any transformational steps. This is the same peace of mind you get when you've organized your files, your desk, or your sock drawer. It can feel good. People are not like socks, though, so making changes in networks requires care to avoid creating hungry ghosts. As Stephen Covey wisely reminded us decades ago in *Seven Habits of Highly Effective People*, you can be efficient with things; you cannot be efficient with people. You will need patience, skill, energy, and perhaps the assistance of experts to do it well.

Even if you haven't felt overloaded, it is still wise to make any major changes carefully and cautiously. Especially if you are at a new stage of life—whether in a career, with the birth of a child, or in retirement—there is still much you do not know and may not be able to anticipate. You will be better prepared for difficult, unknown, or uncertain situations if you have addressed the easy ones first. And remember, as the connector-in-chief among all your networks, the closer a transformational change gets to you and your other primary connections, the more consequential they will be. You'll want to step carefully until you understand how they will ripple throughout the many moving parts in your new life.

That is why at the start of this third ACTSage transformation step, it is important to make changes in support and especially transactional connections before you attempt any primary connections. Those are far easier changes to make than those involving primary connections. In fact, making changes in support and transactional connections might make primary connection changes unnecessary. This is one of the reasons I encouraged you to focus on all your networks instead of focusing on some and ignoring others. You may be pleasantly surprised, for example, how conflicts at home with a spouse or children (primary connections) caused by coming home late or too exhausted to be lovingly engaged might be resolved by engaging staff (support connections) at work. You are certain to have more energy if you set better boundaries so you don't do other's jobs, especially if they are people you are paying for services or are high-maintenance transactional connections. Conflicts at work with a boss or colleagues (primary connections) because you arrive at work late might be resolved by gaining agreement with car pool buddies (support connection) to leave earlier to arrive on time.

Starting with small, easy changes—and especially among support or transactional connections that drain your energy or cause you extra work—will help rebuild the reserves you need to fuel the road ahead. And even small changes can be deceptively transformational. It seems a small thing, but having a Saturday free of errands was life changing for me. Likewise, it seemed like a small change for a friend who cut yearly medical visits in half by finding a family medicine physician to provide the primary care she received from an internist and the women's health care she received from a gynecologist. It wasn't though; it eliminated her need to schedule two sets of appointments, take double the time off work (or use vacation days), wait in two different offices, cover two sets of co-pays and parking fees. It was a bit bigger—but still relatively small—change when she also shifted her children's care from their pediatrician to her family medicine group. In just two small steps, she went from managing three medical groups to managing one.

Consider Important Targets

Although it is best to start with easy targets, by now you may realize there are important risks you should not ignore. Health, safety, and financial welfare are important, especially if someone depends on you. Addressing any risk you identified during those first two ACTSage steps will give you peace of mind now and might make life easier in the future.

As emotionally difficult as it can be to engage advisers to make estate plans, for example, if you are among the 70 percent of Americans without an up-to-date last will or other legal documents in place, you'll be at peace knowing you've protected loved ones. If you are the parent of a college-age child or the adult child of an older parent who does not have similar documents, you and they will have greater peace of mind knowing they have made those plans. Likewise, if your child has serious allergic reactions to a food, it is vital that adults in all your child's networks know. Telling them will give you peace of mind and will protect your child's welfare when you are not there to supervise. If your child is in school or day care, it is important you know their emergency policies, and if they have plans to confirm the identity of any adult at pickup time in the event of an evacuation. If you live distant from elderly parents and learn they have difficulty driving to get groceries, finding a driving or grocery delivery service can make the difference between their independent living at home and costly institutional care.

You might also see important opportunities you don't want to miss. If you need additional education to take your next career step, for instance, you may want to realign your networks to create the time and energy to enroll in an upcoming course. If you're growing a business, there may be upcoming conferences to network with others or trade shows to showcase your products and services it would be unwise to miss. If you live in an area with long waiting lists for good childcare, you might need to register even before your baby is born.

Consider Large Targets

If you have very large networks, there may be ways to simplify your engagements with the people in them. Large extended families, social groups, and workplaces simplify holidays with secret Santa gift-giving in lieu of individual gifts. Homeowners simplify large home-care networks when they downsize from large homes with yards to condominiums or rented properties. People who lead community and volunteer activities simplify large networks when they step away from leadership roles and opt to be participants instead. I am part of a small group of professional women who have maintained social connections for several decades, but it's a supersized effort of no fewer than fifty emails to schedule an outing. We could downsize the effort by using scheduling software!

Seek Guidance

Some transformations are very difficult, especially when they involve primary connections or networks that are very important. In those cases, consider allowing trusted friends, wise counsel, and experts to support you. The consequences of mismanaging transformation with a primary connection—a spouse, child, parent, good friend, or boss—can be grave and damaging for everyone concerned. You may have seen the impact on children when parents divorce or on employees when business partners have major disputes. You may also have seen the impact of unskilled management of important support connections: conflicts with a child's teacher, a parent's neighbor, or an important company vendor, for example.

When your first two ACTSage steps point toward a desirable transformation in a primary connection, a highly valued support connection, or in an important network, it is wise to have guidance. Mental health experts, clergy, life coaches, and business coaches understand the dynamics of those key relationships. They specialize in helping people manage them, can focus on the uniqueness of your situation, and are invaluable.

Facing Resistance

Resistance to change is a fact of life. Regardless of the sincerity of your intentions, you may feel resistance in yourself, and you're certain to feel it from others. The path we walk over many years creates a well-worn trail that leaves deep grooves in our connections, our calendars, our psyches, and even in our brains. Don't be surprised if, when you make a change—especially one involving others—a bit of protest shows up.

Social-Nature Resistance

There are many reasons for this, but I'll mention some related to our social nature. As noted in chapter 2, we are hardwired to connect with others in social groups. Among the most important functions of those groups is survival. Groups do that by sharing food, shelter, and information, and by offering protection from outsiders. Any change you make in yourself—or request of others—can disrupt group dynamics, especially if it appears you may leave the group. To members of the group who are—or fear they will be—left behind, that feels like a survival threat. Fearing for their survival, people in the group won't want you to leave and will take steps to prevent you from doing so.

For example, if you are in groups of sedentary, overweight smokers and decide to adopt a healthy lifestyle and train for a marathon, they may ridicule or reject you for trying. That will make it harder to succeed because you will lack support when the going gets tough, and their rejection will trigger survival fears in you. If you are the first—or the only—one in your family network to go to college, they might do likewise. It is not uncommon for networks to—knowingly or unknowingly, directly or indirectly, subtly or blatantly—sabotage the best diet, fitness, educational achievement, or career-attainment goals.

This dynamic might be why my parents were criticized by their families. As our prospects for a better life improved, their families may have sensed we would leave them behind. I admire my parents for persisting regardless.

Social-Norm Resistance

Social norms create even more subtle resistance dynamics you may feel, as it did for me regarding my student helper. Without realizing it, I created a "social norm" visiting a dry-cleaning establishment on a regular basis over many years, chatting with the owner for a few minutes and asking about her children, whose photos were posted prominently near her cash register. Much to my surprise, when my student helper ran that errand for me, the owner grilled her about why I no longer visited her shop myself. Nor did I realize how strong even unspoken norms could be. I thought I was clever to consider I needed help and generous to give a student a flextime job to make extra money. My social group, however, included working women who did not have household help. They criticized me as indulgent and elitist. Some even suggested I not write about it in this book, hoping to save me additional scorn from people with views like theirs. And though they never outright confronted me, I got disapproving looks from neighbors as my student helper came and went from my property each week.

In this situation, no one's actual survival was at risk. The dry cleaner continued to have my business; she suffered no economic loss. Friends suffered no social loss; in fact, they gained more of my attention. A weekly visit from my student helper caused no more traffic in the neighborhood than if I ran the errands myself. What I encountered in these situations was the social pressure created because I departed from a social norm—one I created and another I didn't know existed.

Social-Taboo Resistance

If you break a connection, you've done something even worse. You've tampered with a social taboo. Family members don't abandon other family members. Friends don't beak connections with friends. To do that would violate the most fundamental social norms that bind us together into our most important survival groups. This helped me understand why the resistance from my dry cleaner (transactional connection) paled by comparison to my attorney's (support connection) hostile reaction when I broke our connection and fired him. Others tell me they have similar experiences with hairdressers, contractors, and financial planners.

Here's why. Initially, many support connections provide good service to win your business, but eventually the quality declines. If this happens, it's gradual. Friendships form from repeated contact, as Sir Robin Dunbar explains. That happens if you talk often, see each other on a regular basis, or work on important projects like wills and estate plans. If you are not careful about boundaries, when you have become friends, you act as a friend would and make allowances for any lapse. Friends do that for friends. You can be more inclined to forgive when they reschedule an appointment. You can be more willing to set a new due date for a project. You can accommodate a hairdresser who keeps you waiting or be too trusting of a financial adviser. I sure did, for many years and with several support connections. A few years into this NetworkSage journey, however, after many missed deadlines to update my will, I fired my attorney. What should have been a conversation to end a business arrangement became a personal attack on me, no doubt to inflict social or psychological discomfort to draw me back in. He reacted like a friend losing a friend, not like a service provider losing a client. In fact, he reacted like an intimate friend. It required third-party intervention—not unlike a custody negotiation—to get my records returned.

Social-Contract Resistance

These dynamics are not only at work with those we know but within a larger social contract context as well. An example is a recent study published in the March 2017 edition of *Sex Roles: A Journal of Research*. It reported on the moral outrage by people across the United States directed to others—even strangers—who are voluntarily childless. According to the study's author, Indiana University professor Leslie Asburn-Nardo, Americans view parenting as a moral imperative. People who choose not to have children cause feelings of anger, disapproval, and disgust, all social tools used to encourage conformity with a social contract.

Dealing with Resistance

Unfortunately, people who resist your transformational efforts won't be aware that their reactions stem from primitive instincts and unwarranted fears that their survival is at risk. They won't know that their reaction will make it harder on you to navigate a transformation you want or need. Clinical neuropsychologist Mario Martinez in *The MindBody Code* describes this dynamic in a poignant story of a small-town country music singer who rises quickly to the top of the music charts. Initially, friends and family basked in the glow of his celebrity. After a while, however, they rejected him, critical that he chose to be away, at work on his career. Their rejection drove him toward drug and alcohol abuse until Martinez showed him the reason for their behavior and he learned to cope with their reactions in other ways.

You may experience something similar. In hopes you will remain connected within a network, people may respond with bizarre behavior, like my attorney trying to bully me into remaining his client. Others tell me they were shamed by their connections. Some say they became a target for gossip. Women tell me their hairdressers—referencing marital infidelity—accuse them of "cheating" if they visit another salon. Not surprisingly, given the strength of some connections, some women feel guilty when they do. In one dramatic example, a client described what happened many years ago when she left a social group behind because a job promotion required she relocate to another state, long before social media would have helped her remain connected. Several months after her move when a group member committed suicide, the others blamed my client, saying her departure was the cause.

The pressure to stay within networks can be so great that the problems created by leaving are greater than the burden of staying, and though this is an unfortunate reality, sometimes it can be better way to go. That was the case for one older woman who was pressured to remain in a bridge club not only by the members but also by her husband. She felt the people in the bridge club were dragging her down, but trying to leave created problems in her family network and social network, and she judged those problems worse than simply going along.

Only time will tell if acceding to the wishes of others will be in this woman's best interests. Given her age and life circumstances, it might, in fact, be the better decision. There are risks of failing to take a transformational step in some situations, however: vulnerability and potentially serious downstream consequences. For example, I've seen parents fail to finalize custody arrangements for their children, fearing family network backlash because they intend to pass up relatives and appoint friends as guardians instead. I know parents who won't ask if there are unsecured guns in the homes where their children play, fearing conflict within their social and community network. I've watched friends sabotage their careers after they were criticized by their spiritual network for their chosen field or financial success.

If you are committed to transformation, you can improve your chances of success if you engage others to gain their support and proactively address their fears if any arise. Whether the change is to learn a new skill, adopt a healthier lifestyle, or stop a bad habit, it will be an ongoing process over many months, years, or even a lifetime. It will require you be self-aware and disciplined, and you are certain to feel some resistance, including in yourself along the way. Just ask anyone who's quit smoking. Just as it requires tremendous thrust for a spaceship to leave the earth's gravitational pull, it takes energy to make changes that depart from the gravitational pull of your own behavior and those of your networks.

When resistance happens to you, use your understanding of how network dynamics can help, as can the advice and support of experts, when necessary. Although it will not eliminate the resistance, it may help you address the real drivers of their fear and yours and help you move forward as smoothly as you can under the circumstances.

Transformation Actions

The destination people reach using this road map is varied. For some, it is a better education for their children, more evenly distributed workloads within a family, or better managed shared-custody arrangements with a former spouse. For others, it is business, income, or career growth. Still others start a nonprofit or better manage the one they have. They arrived using one—or more—of five different types of actions.

Downsize and Simplify

People make their lives easier in some way to redirect their time and energy to more meaningful activities, most of them admitting they had never counted the cost of managing the lifestyles they'd built. Thus, they downsized to-do lists, homes, lifestyles, support services, community engagement, outreach to others, and the number of connections they maintained. In the words of one: "My list of connections looks like someone went speed packing in a cheap suitcase. It might work for a while, but then it all comes apart at the seams at the worst possible time!"

They got help to run errands, as I did, or downsized property to a "just big enough" home, to one with no landscaping to maintain, or opted to rent, ending home ownership altogether. Some discontinued dinner parties in favor of pitch-in potluck picnics. Others shifted entertaining from their home to restaurants, eliminating the effort required to prepare the home, shop for groceries, fix the meal, and clean up afterward. Some resigned from leadership roles in community groups, remaining engaged but opting to not lead. Particularly for those experiencing a sudden change in family needs or work responsibilities, leadership took a toll.

Engage Support Systems

Virtually everyone learned they didn't have adequate support systems at the ready. Feelings of social, legal, health, and economic vulnerability resided just below the surface of their conscious awareness. Traveling this road revealed how it robbed them of peace of mind and created ever-growing worries about the future. To remedy this, they found support services: an attorney, a financial planner, needed support for an elderly parent (for example, a driving service or health care navigator), or various home maintenance and repair services they didn't already have. And in some cases, they replaced existing service providers with ones who were more responsive, more qualified, or nearer to their home or office.

They turned to friends to ask for support to follow physicians' recommendations and better manage a chronic condition. Some reconnected with friends or reached out to form new ones when they realized they had become socially isolated. This happened to parents who saw they connected socially only through their children and to empty nesters whose children were no longer social connectors for them. It also happened to retirees who lost workplace-based connections and to older people who suffered the loss of friends to death. Some people turned to friends, coaches, and counselors to address hungry ghosts and searched for spiritual network connections when they saw they were going it alone, often without realizing they'd drifted away from sources of spiritual support.

Delegate and Communicate

Everyone, not just those with large networks and complicated lives, learned they needed to delegate better. In every case, people realized they had not gathered important information or communicated it to others who might need to know.

As a result, they delegated tasks, rebalanced workloads, and shared information with spouses, with children, and with business partners and employees. They improved communication not only within families but between divorced parents sharing custody so each one had complete contact information for everyone connected in the separate households and neighborhoods, and among siblings caring for elderly parents. Everyone shared vital information with someone else who might need to step in to help, or assembled information and placed it in a location others could find if necessary.

Better Plans and Decisions

With greater awareness about the resources available in their networks, people developed plans to capitalize on connections to address needs. For example, first-time parents explored their networks prior to the child's birth to identify sources of support they would need, especially in the early days when they knew they would be tired. Later, as children grew and had more interactions with people outside the family, parents identified adults responsible for their children. Focusing on their goal to keep children healthy and safe, they made decisions accordingly, for example, declining playdates with children who were not immunized or in homes with guns.

College students accelerated career plans, most often by engaging parents' connections in the field they were considering, interviewing each one to help make career decisions, land better internships, and launch their network in that field. Consultants expanded their customer audience, and sales associates developed better customer-service approaches by understanding their own—and their customer's—networks. Soon-to-be retirees made better retirement plans. In some cases, they identified the important connections they would need to create when they relocated. In other cases, they opted not to relocate when they saw the extent of nearby connections already in place they did not want to lose.

Gain New Insights

Everyone also gains insights, sometimes about others but more often about themselves. For example, one attorney challenged himself to consider his motive when he made referrals to other attorneys: were those based on his social connection or his confidence in their ability to serve the client? Business executives saw they were more tolerant of bad service they received in their personal life than in their work life. They were better stewards of their company's resources than their own. Nearly all working mothers learned how their caregiver role spilled over into all their networks. They spent time and energy on others' needs, risking their work performance and career advancement.

One woman reinterpreted her failed marriage. She saw the failure of some networks to support them and the pressures other networks placed on them were beyond their ability as a young couple to manage without professional help, which no one had suggested and they didn't know to consider. Parents who had encouraged a child to "tough it out" with a bad teacher saw there was more than one year at stake but the rest of his life if the teacher became a hungry ghost. Everyone gained a greater appreciation for the workload to manage a household, children's schedules, and senior care.

What might it mean if everyone could embrace ACTSage? That is the subject of the final chapter.

Key Points

- Start with easy targets, important targets, and those involving support and transactional connections.
- Some changes won't require support, but many changes will.
- Change can disrupt the stability of social groups and result in resistance and sabotage.
- Reach out to experts who understand the dynamics of primary connections and can focus on your unique situation to advise you whenever the need arises.

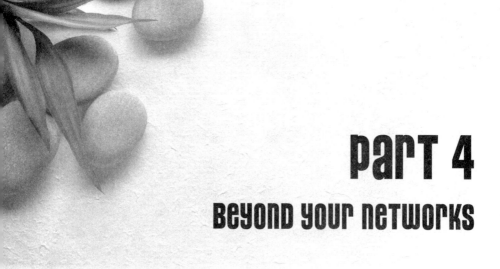

part 4
Beyond your networks

I HOPE THE KNOWLEDGE you gained reading this book has informed and empowered you. I also hope the wisdom you acquired has enlightened you and that this is only the beginning of a new lifelong journey.

If you used this road map as others have, by now you have new ways to look at the past, live in the present, and imagine the future. Like them, you may be making better plans and wiser decisions. Your family, health, education, social, spiritual, household, career, or retirement life is reaping the benefits. You already have greater peace of mind. I say that with confidence because I've seen it happen.

The benefits of NetworkSage insights need not stop with you. This was written for you, but you can use it to help others too, and as promised at the start of this book, this is when I remind you that not only do you *have* pit crews; you are *on* pit crews. Others are depending on you. Sharing these ideas with them can help.

Sharing with primary connections, especially spouses and life partners, can help you build a better life together. Sharing with friends and colleagues can help them understand the requests you make or actions you take, especially when commitments collide and you make an unpopular choice. Sharing this with people in your care can help you learn more about what matters to them and how to activate their networks to help care for them better.

Sharing with a business partner can lead to a NetworkSage partnership. As a manager, you can invite your employees to explore your collective business networks and use everyone's superpower to improve the company's future. In your work life, if you are a support connection providing professional services to clients, especially in medical, legal, and financial arenas that help clients live, work, and succeed better, sharing with them can enrich the services you offer. If you are a policymaker, this can help you build better policies to support the health, education, employment, social, and economic security needs of this nation.

As an experienced NetworkSage, you will see even more ways to do likewise for those you love and care for. As a bonus, it will also make your connection stronger, your parenting or caregiving easier, your client service better, and your statecraft more successful.

Chapter 15
Transform Our Collective Future

The Blueberry Connection

SUNDAY MORNING: PENN STATION, New York, Amtrak waiting area. I was heading home after a weekend in the city when a young woman with a two-year-old sat next to me. Watching them snack on blueberries was delightful. One by one, the mom put a blueberry in the little girl's hand, and she would feed herself. As luck and two-year-old eye-hand coordination would have it, one of the blueberries rolled off the little girl's outstretched palm, bounced across the floor, and came to a stop a few feet away.

"I'll get it," the mom said to me as she nearly leapt from her seat.

"No, I'll get it," I said.

"No, no," she insisted. "I'll get it."

Both of us were still sitting when I turned to face her and, in the best authoritative voice I could muster, said, "Look! *You're* the *mom*. As far as I'm concerned, for all you do, you're a *rock star*! The least I can do is pick up the blueberry." And so, I did.

Heading back to my seat, I caught a glimpse of her; she was tearing

185

up. *Oh my, I was trying to be nice, but look what I've done instead. I've reduced a perfect stranger to tears. How am I going to take the edge off this?*

I told her it bothered me when people ignored women traveling alone with children and didn't reach out to help. I told her about Judy Woodruff's speech at an American Academy of Pediatrics meeting many years before. In those remarks, Woodruff said that when her husband traveled alone with their child, women helped him. When she traveled alone with their child, nobody helped her.

In the few minutes we talked before her train departed, I learned she lived in Washington, DC, and was in New York for a visit. Like so many of her generation, she didn't live near family and didn't have the regular support they could provide. When she offered her business card, I learned that she had a PhD and, in exploring her group's website later, that she was professionally involved in networks supporting at-risk high school students through their college years. The organization helped them complete school, get good jobs, become economically secure, and contribute their many talents to the world.

Our engagement was a transactional connection that lasted for only a few short moments. It happened once; it will never happen again. I've not seen that young woman since, so I don't know the impact it had on her. I do know that it transformed me and was an important milestone in my own NetworkSage journey. A highly educated, competent woman in a responsible, professional leadership position had been nearly reduced to tears by a simple act of kindness from a stranger.

Of course, it wasn't just that simple act of kindness. Though I don't know for certain, I suspect my gesture was meaningful because of her overloaded—and perhaps underresourced—life. Even though I know only a few things about her—and most people I meet—this journey has helped me understand everyone in new ways. In fact, sometimes I think I understand people's lives better than they do. Contemplating that, I'm humbled by the extent of the support we all need to live it well. I am also in awe of everyone, since most people don't have the support they need to achieve their potential but manage to do it regardless. Such is the value of human potential and why I'd like to help make it easier and more likely for everyone.

The difference in my morning and hers that day might be an example. I woke up at a hotel and had only myself to get ready. Room service brought me coffee, a friend bought my breakfast, a doorman hailed a taxi and put my small carry-on in the trunk. On the train home, I'd be able to nap if I wanted to.

By contrast, even if this woman's friends made breakfast, she had herself and her little girl to get dressed that morning and luggage for two to pack. She had a stroller to maneuver and might not have help to load it all into the taxi or unload it again at Penn Station. Her train trip home was two hours longer than mine, and her child may not have napped, so she'd not be able to nap either. On Monday when we arrived at work, I'd feel rejuvenated. Would she? I hoped she would and that other people she saw along the way, even in their transactional encounters with her, offered to help her as a woman traveling alone with a small child.

Be a Village

Fast forward to nearly a year later. In her blog post *To the Mom without a Village*, Chaunie Bruise expresses her gratitude for all the family and friends in the village that support her while, at the same time, wishing for more of one. Many moms I know would agree with her. Some dads I know—especially single dads—agree as well. She questioned, though, if her lack of a village was her fault. She ends her post by reminding mothers who desperately want a village, but don't have one, that they're not alone. You can imagine her raising a glass for a toast: to finding villages, wherever they may be.

I'm not a mom and can't speak for them, but I do think often about parents. I contemplate what life must be like when you are responsible not only for your own networks but also for those of a child, who is totally dependent on the decisions others make, often when you are not there to supervise. I marvel at how well parents adapt to the experience of parenting a first child and to all the new people who enter their lives because of the birthright networks they create. I admire how well they cope with support connections who are not supportive and transactional connections who have different views about childrearing practices and offer advice that is not always welcome, accurate, or helpful.

I worry about them when I hear that marital and job satisfaction declines with the birth of a child, a common experience recently linked to parents losing contact with their own network Then, as the complexity of network management for parents grows with the birth of each new child, I worry again, since they've not just added one more person to the family but an exponential number of connections to manage for each one. I'm concerned even more when a child has a serious illness, a special need, or a special talent. Given their responsibilities and the workload associated with managing children's networks, it is no wonder parents lose touch with their own, as one told me: "The people I talk with most often now are people I did not know before my children were born. I've lost touch with everyone else. I can't keep up."

I'd like to put the shoe on the other foot and suggest that the rest of us not wait until moms or dads reach out. I'd like to suggest that we offer to help before they ask when we can, even in little ways. For those of us who travel, it's a simple thing to hold a door so a mom can maneuver a stroller, to put her luggage in the overhead while she settles in with an infant, or to get her a cup of coffee while she waits at the gate. When we're at home, it's a simple thing to let a parent know we're stopping at the store to pick up dinner and ask if there's something they need. Making that trip with a baby in tow isn't easy; I'm certain they'd be grateful. I'd also like to suggest that it's not the fault of a parent if he or she doesn't have a village. That's about us. We can make the first move and offer some help. We're the village each other needs.

Build a New-Era Village

Villages extend far beyond moms, dads, and blueberries. They include each of us and all those in our networks—and in their networks—and in their networks, and so on. Not just moms but children with special needs or talents, students leaving for college, newlyweds creating a first home, and entrepreneurs starting a business. It includes anyone transitioning from one stage of life to another, everyone facing a personal, family, or career crisis, military families, veterans, and, increasingly, independent-living seniors.

It is in our collective best interest to consciously develop our networks, nurture them, and realize that in this new era they are the villages we need. The increasingly complex world requires it, but there are other reasons as well, including sociocultural changes and the economic impact those create.

High Rates of Mobility

The United States is the most mobile country in the world, geographically separating multiple generations of families and disrupting traditional forms of family, neighborhood, community, career, and spiritual support. No longer do family live nearby—or in multigenerational homes—available for mutual support. An increasing number of grown children relocate for college and jobs, weakening traditional family and village support systems as they leave. In fact, between high school and midlife, 40 percent move an average of 676 miles away from where they were raised. Additionally, 20 percent of adults plan to relocate after retirement, often at distances from the family, friends, and community they know. As exciting as new opportunities might be, relocation separates us from existing support networks. In addition, many people have hypermobile lives with long workday commutes, out-of-town travel, or military deployments and relocations that separate them from important connections.

Changes in Family Structure

Even when families live nearby, radical change in family structure is another reason we need to create new-era villages. Fewer than 20 percent of families are once-married couples with children; more than 80 percent are single-parent, divorced, or remarried families. As told to me by a friend, "My ex-husband is coming to my house to babysit his own kids from our marriage, two kids from my current husband's first marriage—that is, my stepkids—and my toddler from the marriage to my current husband. He's doing that so my current husband and I can take his mother to brunch for Mother's Day. Figure that out? It works for us." They, like one-third of Americans, live in a blended family. In their case, five children, from four parents, from three marriages: three share the same father; three share the same mother.

Living with no family are fourteen million elder orphans. Some never married or had children; others are sole survivors of a family. They cared for others who became ill and died and now have no family left to care for them. Their number will increase exponentially in the future, for several reasons. First, for the first time in US history, single adults outnumber those who are married. Second, the size of the baby boomer generation. Third, the fact that one-third of baby boomers— twenty-five million people—never had children at all.

Women's Employment

Another factor is high rates of employment among women. Far more than half of women over the age of sixteen are now employed outside the home. The majority work full-time, including those who have children, and even newborns. Employment among women over age fifty-five is even higher: 59 percent in 2012, expected to increase to 66 percent by 2020. Mothers, sisters, aunts, and, increasingly, grandmothers are less available for childcare, senior care, and volunteering in schools, hospitals, and community organizations. Work interferes with the traditional roles women have played as the social glue within many networks.

Medical Advancements

Investments made in public health, research, and health care have increased life span by more than three decades. Accompanying longer life, however, are conditions that can require considerable support from others. Some are chronic diseases that are difficult to manage or cause serious complications as people age. This happens not just at the end of life but at the beginning and throughout. Better neonatal care, for example, increases the chances that the one-in-ten babies born with a serious condition will survive but need physical, emotional, and learning disability assistance later. One in twenty working adults is disabled—most often from a workplace injury—unable to see, hear, walk, or live without assistance. Troops wounded in combat are more likely to survive but with chronic pain, mental health, and other disabling conditions that require considerable support.

Baby Boomers

Once again, baby boomers require new societal responses as they age. As seventy-six million people in the boomer generation grow older, they will—as they have at each stage of life—create new demands on all sectors of the economy. Unfortunately, current senior care methods in the United States are already stretched to the breaking point, with waiting lists for all types of services. Even those who can afford paid care may not be able to find it.

Impact on Families

Lacking traditional village and extended-family support, family life is tougher. Among new mothers, 80 percent experience "baby blues," and 20 percent experience perinatal depression. The rate of depression in new fathers is twice that of men who do not have children. Managing chronic conditions like asthma or serious food allergies complicates daily life. During military deployments, families experience increased rates of child abuse and neglect, which impact child health, development, and educational achievement.

Family life also costs more. Parents pay as much as $2,000 per month for infant care and $300 to $1,564 per month (averaging $972 per month) for childcare. They lose, on average, thirteen days of work when infants receive NICU care and bear some of those costs, which can range from $2,000 to 3,000 per day. They lose, on average, between eleven and seventy-three hours of work and incur $300 to $4,000 in medical costs for the less-serious diseases of childhood, like influenza.

When a family member is injured in a civilian job, families incur medical and nonmedical costs exceeding the cost of cancer, only 25 percent of which are covered by worker's compensation. When family members are injured in combat, the average cost of long-term postinjury care is estimated at $2 million, increasingly off-loaded onto families, principally female spouses.

Employed family members who become caregivers supporting older people lose income and incur added health care costs for their own health, both of which carry serious economic penalties. In one study, 74 percent of family members providing care to an older person were employed. Of those, two-thirds made workplace adjustments to do so, resulting, on average, in $142,700 in lost wages, $131,350 in lost Social Security benefits, and $50,000 in lost pension payments. Since caregivers are more likely to suffer illness themselves, their own health care costs increase, not all of which are covered by insurance. Even those who are insured face co-pays and deductibles.

As people age and despite the desire to remain in their current home (87 percent say they do), adapting homes to widen doorways, add grab bars in bathrooms, replace flooring with slip-resistant materials, add wheelchair ramps, and install chair lifts can be expensive. More important and more difficult, however, is finding help to replace the assistance relatives and close friends once provided. This is not a trivial concern, as noted by a recent joint study by Syracuse University

Aging Studies Institute and the Health Foundation of Western and Central New York. That study identified twenty "triggers of decline" that cause vulnerable adults to become frail and require expensive institutional care. Half of those triggers can be prevented by having reliable support connections to help with activities we take for granted as younger people as we manage households, get food, engage socially, and navigate health care. When individuals and families exhaust their ability to remain independent or provide unpaid care at home, the cost of home care is $40,000 (per shift), adult day care is $17,250 per year, the cost of assisted living is $43,200 per year, and the cost of nursing homes is $92,000 and more per year.

The resulting cost and quality-of-life consequence for families place them at risk for health, education, achievement, and financial problems. They can also cause children's behavior problems years later and increase the risk children will be bullied at school. This is not solely a family matter; it impacts all of us economically. As noted by economist Heather Boushey, children are tomorrow's workforce. What happens inside families is just as important to a vibrant economy as what happens inside workplaces.

Impact on Businesses

The ripple effects impact businesses, which bear some of the cost. Family-caregiving employees cost employers 8 percent more than other employees for health care, due to the impact of caregiving on their health: depression, diabetes, hypertension, and pulmonary disease. In total, the differential adds $13 billion to annual employer-paid health costs.

Employers also suffer productivity losses. Not only do parents miss work when children are ill, others providing care do as well. On average, employees caring for an older person miss nearly seven days of work more than other employees. This can create a substantial burden for small or lean businesses with little staff redundancy or when employees hold mission-critical positions. When they are on the job, caregiving employees are also often less present, using work hours to make appointments, coordinate with other caregivers, and manage crises. The combined absenteeism-presenteeism impact is more than $43.7 billion on the gross domestic product of this nation.

Impact on Communities and Governments

Increasingly, communities feel the impact as well as they fill gaps left by the erosion of traditional village support systems. Some of those costs are borne by nonprofit organizations that provide social services to vulnerable people. Other costs are borne by governments and include the funds required to provide services and make infrastructure improvements. Some of those costs are political, as governments adapt public policies and regulations at local, state, and national and in all economic sectors, including childcare, education, public health, health care, housing, transportation, energy, recreation, and even waste management.

For example, geographically distant relatives and other frayed networks can't provide support for those who need help to get food, care for children, or access health care. Public safety-net programs must do that. Stepping into that gap, public funds are used for school-based programs, including food for thirty-one million children who receive free or low-cost lunches and after-school snacks. Funds are required for pre-K classes that provide childcare, health care, mental health care, and oral health care. Nurses ride school buses transporting children with special needs to monitor their conditions and manage medications. Some schools employ nurses; those without a nurse train other staff to deal with ADD, depression, diabetes, emergency care, serious allergies, infectious diseases, epilepsy, tracheostomy, medication management, and obesity.

Communities also provide safety net transportation for older people who can no longer drive. The national cost of improving the transportation infrastructure is $4.2 billion. Local governments, community organizations, and rural areas will bear the brunt of those costs. Local municipal waste departments incur costs when they make special sanitation arrangements for older people who can no longer place household waste containers at curbs for pickup. Vulnerable, disabled, or older adults in a community require special considerations during natural disasters. When people and families exhaust their resources and someone becomes eligible for nursing home coverage through the state's Medicaid program, the cost—borne by a state—is among the highest.

Adapting public policies and regulations can be costly. Government leaders at all levels invest time, funds for studies, and often political capital. For example, many current zoning and building codes prevent building of smaller, more affordable homes or placing "granny pods" on property owned by adult children to ease caregiving. Current local tax structures and municipal service payment systems are ill adapted to growing numbers of seniors who fail to manage finances well. Some forget or are unaware they must pay relatively small water or tax assessment bills until their homes are sold at auction—even without prior notice—to pay the bill. Missteps such as this have catalyzed outrage and political backlash in some states.

New Lessons Learned

Those factors are a perfect storm that supports the rationale to build new-era villages to help all of us today and in the future. At one time, that was my academic or policy concern. Now it's deeply personal, and my experiences resonate with those of people everywhere who have older relatives. Concerns about children, households, and careers have not gone away. On occasion, however, those have been eclipsed by the demands of caregiving for older relatives.

For people in my family, this is a new experience. We have no history of age-related disability or decline to inform—or warn—us. Aging was never dinnertime conversation because serious illnesses did not befall us. Everyone lives long lives, vibrantly engaged until the end. My maternal grandmother is an example. At the age of seventy-three, she sold her home in the Midwest and relocated to North Dakota. She started her last career there, remaining active until she died—at work—on her ninety-third birthday. My brother and sister-in-law were hospice volunteers for decades, and I visited church members in nursing homes. That helped us understand some of the issues. I understood others from my work in health policy and knew the statistics about the millions of people who needed care and the billions of dollars required to provide it. Then my mom became suddenly, seriously, and mysteriously ill.

Four decades in health care hadn't prepared me to deal with the maze of providers, the uncertainties of her condition, the long waits between appointments and referrals, or the failure of physicians to take her concerns seriously. Worse, she lived a thousand miles away, and it took an entire day's travel to reach her. Though my brother and sister-in-law live nearby and that has always been a comfort to me, during some of the most harrowing days of her illness, they were out of the country and could not be reached. NetworkSage though I may be in some ways, I had not taken the steps to learn about my mom's networks or connect to the important people in them. I managed with contact information for one neighbor, who, thankfully, was incredibly helpful. My mom counts this neighbor as one of her best friends, and the strength of their connection fueled her willingness to step in when I could not, saving Mom's life more than once.

Initially, Mom resisted when I offered to engage a group of nurse case managers in my own network to support us, but eventually she acquiesced. They intervened and found a clinical study for an experimental treatment that, happily, worked. Today, she is fully recovered. That was a hard road, but like the others I've traveled, the lessons learned have helped people since. It reinforced my views about the value of building good networks throughout each stage of life, to prepare for crises, and especially without the backup support traditional villages once offered.

Like too many of us, she had prepared for the eventuality of her death, not for the reality of a much longer life. Her new understanding about networks is changing that. She saw the size of the network required to maintain her home and explored—but rejected—assisted living. She chose instead to make improvements to her home to help her remain there. She saw that her social network was good but small, so she joined the single's club to find friends for exercise and social events. This proved to be wise when, soon after she recovered from her illness, three of her four best friends—including the one who helped when she was ill—announced they were relocating to be near their adult children.

She's a NetworkSage now. She has completed the ACTSage steps, reaffirmed her goal to live independently, and is working toward that in many ways. In addition to those I've mentioned, she got a trainer and is weight-training to restore the strength she lost during those months of illness. She water-walks to improve her fitness. Important from my perspective, she gave us contact information for everyone in her networks.

Like so many of the other network-related insights on this journey, my mom's illness showed me something that was hiding in plain sight, and it is this, the theme of this chapter: the need is real, and the time is right to create new-era support systems.

Envision the Future

New-era villages would assure everyone—as individuals, families, businesses, local communities, states, and the nation—prospers in today's ever-changing world. In this vision of the future, parents would build a better family life. People in the workforce would achieve success, satisfaction, and career achievement. Empowered older adults would live independently, age well in place, maintain their health and quality of life, and find meaning in creative contributions they make at this stage of life.

Family, friends, and caregivers would be able to provide better, more appropriate—but less burdensome—support for others in need. Public and private, health, education, and social service organizations and the professionals who work within them would be more efficient and effective. Businesses would better optimize employee productivity and achieve commercial and financial success. Governments would be better able to address the economic, policy, and regulatory challenges created by our rapidly changing world.

Every NetworkSage is proof that with ingenuity and commitment, people can build new-era villages to support them. If they can, you can too. If enough of us do, our interlocking networks will provide ever-stronger support for us all. What you've explored in these pages can help. Your understanding of networks put to good use can transform life as we know it, which is why I'm certain that this is not the end of the road. It's only the beginning.

How can this be done? There are as many ways as there are people who will give it a try. I know that's true because, in the years since I began this exploration, people have done it. I am no longer surprised when someone tells me they found a new use for the discoveries they made as a NetworkSage. If our lives and human potential are canvases without limits, networks may well be a new kind of paint.

You will have other ideas too, I'm sure. As you do, I'd like to know. I'd like to hear your stories and encourage you to share them to enrich the experience for every person who gives this a try. So, come join the community and become a NetworkSage too.

Your Life, Your Way

Your networks are your superpower, and ACTSage is a power tool, but that's not all. What I said at the start is worth repeating: human potential is virtually unlimited, far from being exhausted, and ready to be realized. I believe you to be a vitally important and truly unique individual, the pinnacle of centuries of human experience, poised to leave a distinctive imprint only you can make.

As I imagine you reading this, I don't see you there alone. I see all your ancestors reading over your shoulder. Likewise, as I write, mine are peering over mine. We are heirs to their wisdom. We benefit from the world they created for us, and we can create an even better one for those who come after.

As you work to chart a new course, get ahead, navigate a big change, share your abundance, or triumph over a challenge, as a NetworkSage, I know you can succeed.

The superheroes I admire are not only the ones in movies. As a NetworkSage, you are one too.

Key Points

- Traditional village support has eroded.
- Not just family networks but others have been impacted by mobility and social change.
- These changes contribute to stress for everyone, with some long-term consequences.
- Individuals, families, businesses, and governments incur added costs.
- The opportunity is ripe to build new-era villages of support.

references

Chapter 3—Connections Fuel Your Future

American Sociological Association. "Greater academic achievement in high school increases likelihood of moving away" (August 22, 2016). www.sciencedaily.com/releases/2016/08/160822083252.htm.

Baker, David A., and Guillermo Perez Algorta. "The Relationship Between Online Social Networking and Depression: A Systematic Review of Quantitative Studies." *Cyberpsychology, Behavior, and Social Networking* 19, no. 11 (2016): 638. doi:10.1089/cyber.2016.0206.

Barnes, Lisa L., Carlos F. Mendes de Leon, Robert S. Wilson, Julia L. Bienias, Denis A. Evans. "Social Resources and Cognitive Decline in a Population of Older African Americans and Whites." *Neurology* 63 (2004): 2322–26. [PubMed: 15623694].

Beck, Kenneth H., and Samantha Watters. "Characteristics of college students who text while driving: Do their perceptions of a significant other influence their decisions? Transportation Research Part F: traffic." *Psychology and Behaviour* 37 (2016). doi:10.1016/j.trf.2015.12.017.

Bucholz, E. M., K. M. Strait, R. P. Dreyer, M. Geda, E. S. Spatz, H. Bueno, J. H. Lichtman, G. D'Onofria, J. A. Spertus, H. M. Krumholz. "Effect of Lowe Perceived Social Support on Health Outcomes in Young Patients with Acute Myocardial Infarction: Results from the VIRGO (Variation in Recovery: Role of Gender on Outcomes of Young AMI Patients)." *Journal of the American Heart Association* 3, no. 5 (2014): e001252. doi:10.1161/JAHA.114.001252.

Cacioppo. *Loneliness: Human Nature and the Need for Social Connection.* W.W. Horton & Co., 2009.

Chopik, William J. "The Benefits of Social Technology Use Among Older Adults Are Mediated by Reduced Loneliness. Cyberpsychology." *Behavior and Social Networking* (2016). doi:10.1089/cyber.2016.0151.

Christakis, N. A., and J. H. Fowler. "The Spread of Obesity in a Large Social Network over 32 years." *N Engl J Med* 357 (2007): 370–9.

Christakis, Nicholas, and James Fowler. "Social contagion theory: examining dynamics social networks and human behavior." *Statistics in Medicine* 32 (2013): 556–577.

Cohen, S. A., and S. Gössling. A darker side of hypermobility, Environment and Planning A (in press) (2015).

Cohen, Sheldon, William J. Doyle, David P. Skoner, Bruce S. Rabin, Jack M. Gwaltney Jr. "Social Ties and Susceptibility to the Common Cold." *Journal of the American Medical Association* (1997).

Cornwell, Erin York. "Household Disorder, Network Ties, and Social Support in Later Life." *Journal of Marriage and Family* 78 (2016): 871–889. doi:10.1111/jomf.12299.

Cote-Lussier, Carolyn, and Caroline Fitzpatrick. "Feelings of Safety at School, Socioemotional Functioning, and Classroom Engagement." *Journal of Adolescent Health* 58, no. 5 (2016): 543. doi:10.1016/j.jadohealth.2016.01.003.

Dunbar, Robin. *How Many Friends Does One Person Need: Dunbar's Number and Other Evolutionary Quirks.* Cambridge, MA: Harvard University Press, 2010.

Dyble et al. "Network of Food Sharing Reveal the Functional Significance of Multilevel Sociality in Two Hunter-Gatherer Groups." *Current Biology* (2016). doi:10.1016/j.cub.2016.05.064.

Esipova, N., A. Pugliese, J. Ray. "81 Million Adults Worldwide Migrate Within Countries. U.S. one of the most mobile countries in the world." Gallup Poll, May 15, 2013.

Feeney, B. C., and N. L. Collins. "A New Look at Social Support: A Theoretical Perspective on Thriving through Relationships." *Personality and Social Psychology Review* (2014). doi:10.1177/1088868314544222.

Flora, Carlin. *Friendfluence: The Surprising Way Friends Make Us Who We Are.* Random House, 2015.

Hall, J. A. "When is social media use social interaction? Defining mediated social interaction." *New Media & Society* (2016). doi:10.1177/1461444816660782.

Heikkinen, Riitta-Liisa, and Markku Kauppinen. "Depressive Symptoms in Late Life: A 10-Year Follow-Up." *Archives of Gerontology and Geriatrics* 38 (2004): 239–50. [PubMed: 15066310].

Hobbs, W.R., Burke, M.K. "Connective recovery in social networks after the death of a friend." *Nature Human Behaviour* 1 (2017): 0092. doi:10.1038/s41562-017-0092.

Hobson, N.M., Gino, F., Norton, M.I., Inzlicht, M. "When Novel Rituals Lead to Intergroup Bias: Evidence from Economic Games and Neurophysiology." *Psychological Science* (2017): 095679761769509. doi:10.1177/0956797617695099.

Hold-Lunstad, J., T. B. Smith, M. Baker, T. Harris, D. Stephenson. "Loneliness and Social Isolation as Risk Factors for Mortality, A Meta-Analytic Review." *Perspectives on Psychological Science* 10, no. 2: 227–237. https://doi.org/10.1177/1745691614568352.

LeRoy, A.S., Murdock, K.W., Jaremka, L.M., Loya, A., Fagundes, C.P. Loneliness Predicts Self-Reported Cold Symptoms After A Viral Challenge. *Health Psychology*, 2017.

http://www.bankrate.com/finance/retirement/survey-who-wants-to-retire-elsewhere.aspx.

https://www.ted.com/talks/nicholas_christakis_the_hidden_ influence_of_social_networks?language=en. and https://www.ted. com/talks/nicholas_christakis_how_social_networks_predict_ epidemics?language=en.

Johnson, Katerina V.-A., and Robin I. M. Dunbar. "Pain tolerance predicts human social network size." Nature, *Scientific Reports* 6, article number 25267 (April 28, 2016). doi:10.1038/srep25267.

Kaizad, Kohyar, Scott E. Seibert, Marka L. Kraimer. "Psychological contract breach and employee innovation: A conservation of resources perspective." *Journal of Occupational and Organizational Psychology* 87, no. 3 (2014): 535. doi:10.111/joop.12062.

Kanai, B. Bahame, R. Roylance, G. Rees. "Online social network size is reflected in human brain structure. Proceedings of the Royal Society B." *Biological Sciences* (2011). doi:10.1098/rspb.2011.1959.

Kanduada, A. S., C. W. O'Neal, T. K. Lee. "The Health Impact of Upward Mobility: Does Socioeconomic Attainment Make Youth More Vulnerable to Stressful Circumstances?" *Journal of Youth and Adolescence* 45, no. 2 (2015): 271. doi:10.1007/s10964-015-03797-7.

Lui, H., and L. Waite. "Bad Marriage, Broken Heart? Age and Gender Differences in the Link between Marital Quality and Cardiovascular Risks Among Older Adults." *Journal of Health and Social Behavior* 55, no. 4 (2014): 403. doi:10.1177.0022146514556893.

Maxwell, Lorraine E. "School building condition, social climate, student attendance and academic achievement: A mediation model." *Journal of Environmental Psychology* 46 (2016): 206. doi:10.1016/j.jenvp.2016.04.009.

Monin, Joan, Margaret Doyle, Becca Levy, Rihard Schulz, Terri Fried, Trace Kershaw. "Spousal Associations Between Frailty and Depressive Symptoms: Longitudinal Findings from the Cardiovascular Health Study." *Journal of the American Geriatrics Society* 64, no. 4 (2016): 824. doi:10.111/jgs.14023.

Pachucki, M. A., P. F. Jacques, N. A. Christakis. "Social Network Concordance in Food Choices Among Spouses, Friends and Siblings." *Am J Public Health* 101 (2011): 2170–2177. doi:10.2105/AJPH.2011.300282).

Paton, Douglas, and Melanie Irons. "Communication, Sense of Community, and Disaster Recovery: A Facebook Case Study." *Frontiers in Communication* 1 (2016). doi:10.3389/fcomm.2016.0004.

Pendry, L. F., and J. Salvatore. "Individual and social benefits of online discussion forums." *Computers in Human Behavior* 50 (2015): 211. doi:10.1016/j.chb.2015.03.067.

R.I.M. "Do online social media cut through the constraints that limit the size of offline social networks?" *Royal Society Open Science* 3, no. 1 (2016): 150292. doi:10.1098/rsos.150292.

Ramey, D. M. "The Social Structure of Criminalized and Medialized School Discipline." *Sociology of Education* 88, no. 3 (2015): 181. doi:10.1177/0038040715587114.

Rosenquist, J. N., J. H. Fowler, N. A. Christakis. "Social Network Determinants of Depression." *Molecular Psychiatry* (2011).

Sear, Rebecca, and Ruth Mace. "Who Keeps Children Alive? A review of the effects of kin on child survival." *Evolution and Human Behavior* 29, no. 1: 1–18, doi:10.1016/j.evolhumbehav.2007.10.001.

Seligman, Martin. *Flourish: A Visional New Understanding of Happiness and Well-Being.* Simon and Schuster Digital Sales Inc., 2011.

Wansink, Brian. *Slim by Design: Mindless Eating Solutions for Everyday Life.* William Morrow, 2014.

Xiao, N.G., Wu, R., Quinn, P.C., Liu, S., Tummeltshammer, Natasha, K.S., Kirkham, Z., Ge, L., Pascalis, O., Le, K. "Infants Rely More on Gaze Cues from Own-Race Than Other-Race Adults for Learning Under Uncertainty." *Child Development* (2017). doi:10.1111/cdev.12798.

Chapter 4—Family Networks

http://www.pewsocialtrends.org/2010/11/18/the-decline-of-marriage-and-rise-of-new-families/.

Chapter 5—Health and Vitality Networks

Bloom, D. E., and D. Canning. "The health and wealth of nations." *Science* 287, no. 5456 (2000): 1207–1209, as cited in Mirvis, D. M., and D. E. Bloom. "Population Health and Economic Development in the US." *JAMA* 300, no. 1 (2008): 94.

Britain's Got Talent. https://www.youtube.com/watch?v=RxPZh4AnWyk.

Carney, Maria T., Janic Fijiwaa, Brian E. Emmert Jr., Tara A. Liberman, Barbara Paris. "Elder Orphans Hiding in Plain Sight: A Growing Vulnerable Population." *Current Gerontechnology and Geriatrics Research*, article 4723250 (2016). http://dx.doi.org/10.1155/2016/4723250.

Eagly, A. H., R. D. Ashmore, M. G. Makhijani, L. C. Longo. "What is beautiful is good, but … : A meta-analytic review of research on the physical attractiveness stereotype." *Psychological Bulletin* 110 (1991): 109–128.

French, M. T., I. Popovici, P. K. Robins, and J. F. Homer. "Personal traits, cohabitation, and marriage." *Social Science Research* 45 (2014): 184–199.

Gunaydin, G., E. Selcuk, V. Zayas. "Impressions Based on a Portrait Predict, 1-Month Later, Impressions Following a Live Interaction." *Social Psychological and Personality Science* (2016). doi:10.1177/1948550616662123.

Howson, C. P., H. V. Fineberg, B. R. Bloom. "The pursuit of global health: the relevance of engagement for developed countries." *Lancet* 351 (1998): 586.

https://www.census.gov/topics/families.html

https://www.aap.org/en-us/about-the-aap/aap-press-room/pages/assafcaregivingyouthsatfinal.pdf.

Lereya, Suzet Tanya, and Dieter Wolke. "Prenatal family adversity and maternal mental health and vulnerability to peer victimization at school." *Journal of Child Psychology and Psychiatry* (2012). doi:10.1111/jcpp.12012.

López, Daniel López, Marta Elena Losa Iglesias, Ricardo Becerro de Bengoa Vallejo, Patricia Palomo López, Ángel Morales Ponce, Alfredo Soriano Medrano, Francisco Alonso Tajes. "Optimal choice of footwear in the elderly population." *Geriatric Nursing* 36, no. 6 (2015): 458. doi:10.1016/j.gerinurse.2015.07.003.

Mack, D., and D. Rainey. "Female applicants' grooming and personnel selection." *Journal of Social Behavior and Personality* 5 (1990): 399–407.

Mirvis, D. M., and D. E. Bloom. "Population Health and Economic Development in the US." *JAMA* 300, no. 1 (2008): 94–95.

Robinson, Monique, Eugen Mattes, Wendy Oddy, Craig Pennell, Anke van Eekelen, Neil Mclean, Peter Jacoby, Jianghong Li,

Nicholas de Klerk, Stephen Zubrick, Fiona Stanley, and John Newnham. "Prenatal stress and risk of behavioral morbidity from age 2 to 14 years: The influence of the number, type, and timing of stressful life events." *Development and Psychopathology* 23 (2011): 155–168.

Sachs, J. D. "Macroeconomics & Health: Investing in Health for Economic Development." *WHO Publications* (2001): 1–210.

World Bank. *World Development Report: Investing in Health*, iii: 17–37. Oxford University Press, 1993.

Yusuf, S., K. Nabeshima, W. Ha. "Income and Health in Cities: the Messages from Stylized Facts." *J Urban Health: Bulletin of the NY Acad Med* 18, no. 1 (2007): i35.

Chapter 6—Education and Enrichment Networks

Gibbs, Benjamin G., Lance D. Erickson, Midaela J. Durfur, Aaron Miles. "Extracurricular associations and college enrollment." *Social Science Research* (2014). doi:10.1016/j.ssresearch.2014.08.013.

Gottfried, M.A. "Linking Getting to School with Going to School." *Educational Evaluation and Policy Analysis* (April 2017). doi:10.3102/0162373717699472.

Justice, Laura M., Yaacov Petscher, Christopher Schatschneider, Andrew Mashburn. "Peer Effects in Preschool Classrooms: Is Children's Language Growth Associated With Their Classmates' Skills?" *Child Development* (2011). doi:10.1111/j.1467-8624.2011.01665.x.

Meyer, L. E., and M. M. Ostrosky. "Impact of an Affective Intervention on the Friendships of Kindergarteners With Disabilities." *Topics in Early Childhood Special Education* (2015). doi:10.1177/0271121415571419.

Chapter 7—Spiritual Networks

Pew Research Center. "America's Changing Religious Landscape." May 12, 2015.

Chapter 8—Social and Community Networks

Achor, Shawn. *Before Happiness: The 5 Hidden Keys to Achieving Success, Spreading Happiness, and Sustaining Positive change.* Crown Business, 2013.

Chapter 10—Home and Personal Affairs Networks

http://www.nytimes.com/interactive/2014/upshot/buy-rent-calculator. html.

https://nmhc.org/Content.aspx?id=4708.

SEI. 2014. Used with permission.

Chapter 12—ACTSage Step 1: Awareness

Martinez, Mario. *The MindBody Code: How to Change the Beliefs that Limit Your Health, Longevity, and Success.* Sounds True, 2014.

Mind Mapping tools include: Buzan's iMindMap™, Mind Tools™, NodexL, Kumu, GenoGram™, XMind, MindMeister, TouchGraph.

Chapter 14—ACTSage Step 3: Transformation

Ashburn-Nardo, Leslie. "Parenthood as a Moral Imperative? Moral Outrage and the Stigmatization of Voluntarily Childfree Women and Men." Sex Roles 76, no. 5–6 (2016): 393. doi:10.1007/s11199-016-0606-1.

Chapter 15—Transform Our Collective Future

American College of Obstetrics and Gynecology. "Treatment Guidelines for Depression During Pregnancy and Postpartum Depression." January 2016.

Jeon, S., Pohl, R.V. "Health and work in the family: Evidence from spouses' cancer diagnoses." *Journal of Health Economics* 52, no. 1 (2017). doi:10.1016/j.jhealeco.2016.12.008.

American Public Transportation Association. "Funding the Public Transportation Needs of an Aging Population." http://www.apta.com/resources/reportsandpublications/Documents/TCRP_J11_Funding_Transit_Needs_of_Aging_Population.pdf.

American Sociological Association. "Greater academic achievement in high school increases likelihood of moving away." August 22, 2016. www.sciencedaily.com/releases/2016/08/160822083252.htm.

Beach, S. R., R. Schulz, J. L. Yee, S. Jackson. "Negative and positive health effects of caring for a disabled spouse: Longitudinal findings from the Caregiver Health Effects Study." *Psychology & Aging* 15, no. 2 (2000): 259–271. doi:10.1037//0882-7974.15.2.259.

Bostwick, R., K. Dermady, S. Furtney et al. "Aging Well in Place: 'Start a Conversation' to provide vulnerable seniors and their non-professional caregivers with a tool to support aging well in place." Health Foundation of Western and Central New York Health Leadership Fellows Group Project: Cohort V Team Liszt. May 2016.

Boushey, H. *Finding Time: The Economics of Work-Life Conflict*. Harvard University Press, 2016.

Brown, M. T., and K. Williams. "Policy Brief: Identifying Interventions to Address Triggers of Decline in Vulnerable Older Adults."

Syracuse University Aging Studies Institute. March 10, 2016. http://asi.syr.edu.

Esipova, N., A. Pugliese, J. Ray. "81 Million Adults Worldwide Migrate within Countries. U.S. one of the most mobile countries in the world." Gallup Poll. May 15, 2013.

Family Caregiver Alliance. "Fact Sheet: Selected Caregiver Statistics, Impact on Working Caregivers." Updated November 2012. https://www.caregiver.org/caregiver-statistics-work-and-caregiving

Gallup. "Caregiving Costs the US Economy $25.2 in Lost Productivity." http://www.gallup.com/poll/148670/caregiving-costs-economy-billion-lost-productivity.aspx.

Haley, W. E., L. A. LaMonde, B. Han, A. M. Burton, R. Schonwetter. "Predictors of depression and life satisfaction among spousal caregivers in hospice: Application of a stress process model." *Journal of Palliative Medicine* 6 (2003): 215–224.

Harmell, A. L., E. A. Chattillion, S. K. Roepke, B. T. Mausbach. "A review of the psychobiology of dementia caregiving: A focus on resilience factors." *Current Psychiatry Reports* 13, no. 3 (2011): 219–224. doi:10.1007/s11920-011-0187-1.

http://mchb.hrsa.gov/chusa13/perinatal-health-status-indicators/p/infant-morbidity.html.

http://watson.brown.edu/costsofwar/costs/human/veterans.

http://www.babycenter.com/0_how-much-youll-spend-on-childcare_1199776.bc.

http://www.census.gov/hhes/families/data/cps2014A.html.

https://www.babble.com/parenting/to-the-mom-without-a-village/.

https://www.cbo.gov/sites/default/files/113th-congress-2013-2014/
workingpaper/49837-Casualties_WorkingPaper-2014-08_1.pdf.

https://www.census.gov/newsroom/releases/archives/miscellaneous/
cb12-134.html.

https://www.dol.gov/wb/stats/stats_data.htm.

https://www.ssa.gov/policy/docs/ssb/v65n4/v65n4p31.html.

Lereya, ST, and D. Wolke. "Prenatal family adversity and maternal
mental health and vulnerability to peer victimization at school."
Journal of Child Psychology and Psychiatry (2012). doi:10.1111/
jcpp.12012.

Marak, C. "How to Relieve the Economic Strains of the Aging
Population." Huffington Post. July 15, 2016. http://www.
huffingtonpost.com/entry/how-to-address-the-economic-strains-
of-the-aging-population_us_57893f7fe4b0cbf01e9fbc42.

MetLife. "Study of Working Caregivers and Employer Health Care
Costs." http://www.caregiving.org/wp-content/uploads/2011/06/
mmi-caregiving-costs-working-caregivers.pdf.

National Opinion Research Center. "Long term care in America:
Expectations and realities." May 2014. Retrieved from
http://www.longtermcarepoll.org/PDFs/LTC%202014/AP-
NORC-Long-Term%20Care%20in%20America_FINAL%20
WEB.pdf.

Ortega-Sanchez, I. R., N. A. Molinari, G. Fairbrother et al. "Indirect,
out-of-pocket and medical costs from influenza-related illness in
young children." *Vaccine* 30, no. 28 (2012): 4175–4181.

Robinson, M., E. Mattes, W. Oddy et. al. "Prenatal stress and risk of behavioral morbidity from age 2 to 14 years: The influence of the number, type, and timing of stressful life events." *Development and Psychopathology* 23 (2011): 155–168.

realize your network superpower
key points

Preface

- Human potential is virtually unlimited, and the value of human capital is underappreciated.
- As humans, we need to connect with others, yet there are limits to doing that well.
- You must be in the driver's seat, not out of selfishness but born of your uniqueness and your role as connector-in-chief.
- A network information architecture helps organize networks for better recall of the people in them.
- ACTSage is a three-step process to become aware of your connections, gain clarity about your needs, and transform your networks.
- You and any road maps you use must be flexible to adapt to your circumstances and the world as both change.

Introduction

- Busy people need support from others.
- Being overloaded places your valuable human capital at risk.
- Being underresourced as well risks harm to those you care for.
- Support to help you—pit crews—is there, hiding in plain sight.

Part 1—Superheroes, Pit Crews, and Networks

Chapter 1—Superhero to the Rescue

- Human potential is nearly unlimited.
- Human capital—yours and others'—is your highest-value asset.
- Networks of people support every aspect of your life, not just your careers.
- You are in others' networks, supporting them. To do it well, you need support.

Chapter 2—Connections Fuel Your Future

- You are hardwired to connect with others.
- The quality of your connections determines your health, wealth, success, and happiness.
- Social complexity is far greater in today's world.
- There is a limit to how many connections you can maintain and manage well.
- You can engage with virtual-life connections on social media, but you need face-to-face connections as well.

Chapter 3—You Belong in the Driver's Seat

- Claim your rightful place at the center of your networked life.
- Appreciate your uniqueness and own connector-in-chief role.
- Distinguish among the primary, support, and transactional connections you have with others.
- Making distinctions is not discrimination but a way to decide whether and where to spend time and energy and how to decide between competing commitments.

Part 2—Exploring Network Territory

Chapter 4—Family Networks

- This network provides you with the care you need as a child and creates all five birthright networks.
- Your connections in these networks change as you mature, but you never outgrow the need for what they provide.
- Today's definition of a family has changed and is far more varied than in the past.
- Today's families are smaller, separated by career and retirement mobility, and disrupted, with once-married couples with children no longer the norm.
- A large—and growing—group of seniors have no family support at all.

Chapter 5—Health and Vitality Networks

- This network helps you live a long and healthy life.
- Good health improves personal, family, business, and national wealth.
- A good appearance enhances social standing and economic security.
- Primary health, dental, and vision care are essential.
- Specialist, institutional, and at-home care support are also commonly necessary.

Chapter 6—Education and Enrichment Networks

- This network assures you learn the facts and skills valued by society.
- It fosters social network connections and transmits social norms, disadvantaging those who do not conform.
- Not just teachers but also fellow students have an impact on social and academic success in school.

- Modern technology and global communications support increasingly available personal education and enrichment opportunities for people of all ages.
- This network supports social and community network connections, which benefit people of all ages.

Chapter 7—Spiritual Networks

- This network supports humankind's search for meaning and solace, especially in the face of events that threaten survival.
- Disconnecting from religious congregations is a relatively new and growing trend.
- The number of people in the United States who say they are "spiritual, not religious" outnumbers any single religious group.
- Modern technology and global communications support access to all the world's religious and spiritual traditions.

Chapter 8—Social and Community Networks

- This network helps you move safely and easily as you engage in the world outside your family.
- It grows larger as you grow, encompassing friends, friends of friends, and people in distant places.
- It changes as other networks and life stages or life events change, shrinking or growing as your needs require.
- You need face-to-face engagement with real people. Social media engagement in a virtual world is not sufficient.

Chapter 9—Career Networks

- This network supports you as you express your talents and achieve career aspirations.
- It helps you build new skills and economic security.

- Success in this network is impacted by the strengths and weaknesses of other networks.
- Changes in today's workplaces require greater self-management of career and other networks.

Chapter 10—Home and Personal Affairs Networks

- This network supports your need to manage, protect, and grow your property and other assets, including digital assets.
- It is the source of expert advice concerning your legal and financial affairs, providing you with the peace of mind that you and loved ones are protected.
- Coming of age is a process, not an event, beginning earlier than most people believe.
- It is wise to provide important contact information to another person, or to keep it in a place they can find, so they can help if the need arises.

Chapter 11—Ghost Networks

- Most of the people who were once important in your life may no longer be present.
- Even brief and superficial encounters can leave a lasting impact.
- Later in life is a time most people explore the impact of ghosts in their lives.
- Inexplicably strong reactions to people and events can signal the presence of forgotten ghosts.

Part 3—How to ACTSage

Chapter 12—ACTSage Step 1: Awareness

- Important connections are hiding in plain sight.
- A list, organization chart, or mind map can help you find and visualize connections.

- Aim for a good-enough list, and expect network crush.
- Include all networks and refine contact details later.

Chapter 13—ACTSage Step 2: Clarity

- Gain greater clarity by focusing on your networks, connections, life events, risks, and plans.
- Create an at-a-glance enhancement of your list, organization chart, or mind map with colors and symbols meaningful to you.
- Assess the strength and readiness of your current connections to provide the support you need, including in the important roles you have supporting others.
- Identify connections that are missing, and develop plans to add them.
- Determine if there are changes or disconnections from others that need to take place, and develop plans to do that.

Chapter 14—ACTSage Step 3: Transformation

- Start with easy targets, important targets, and those involving support and transactional connections.
- Some changes won't require support, but many changes will.
- Change can disrupt the stability of social groups and result in resistance and sabotage.
- Reach out to experts who understand the dynamics of primary connections and can focus on your unique situation to advise you whenever the need arises.

Part 4—Beyond Your Networks

Chapter 15—Transform Our Collective Future

- Traditional village support has eroded.
- Not just family networks but others have been impacted by mobility and social change.

- These changes contribute to stress for everyone, with some long-term consequences.
- Individuals, families, businesses, and governments incur added costs.
- The opportunity is ripe to build new-era villages of support.

acknowledgments

It takes a pit crew to write a book too.

Right from the start and at each step along the way, I could count on Nancy and John Bloeser, Ira Brenner, MD, Nancy Zatzman of ProtoType Services, and Diana Long for just about anything I needed.

Also throughout, I was privileged by those hundreds of people who trusted me with their stories, personal insights, and often private and painful frustrations.

Some helped at critical moments: Judy Weintraub of SkillBites, Candy Roberts of QuantumThink, my just-like-family brother Ed Cosgrove, longtime colleague Jonathan Peck of the Institute for Alternative Futures, and Meryl Comer, whose caregiving and grace will always be a source of inspiration. They read drafts, offered critiques, and challenged word choices, all the while encouraging me to keep going. Joining them were Charles Aswad, MD, Nancy Aureli, Alice Bast, Robin Bender-Stevens, Gary Brunson, Sara Canuso, Marlaina Capes, Robin Cortese, Rita Davis, Doug Durand, Linda Elam, Alex Georgio, Phillip Gerbino, Crystal Gornto, Sharon Hackney-Robinson, George Hardy, Charles Inlander, Stephanie Lee Jackson, David Kosar, Bruce Lamont, Joann Lenweaver, Susan Neunaber, Peggy Ogdin, Erin Owen, Robert Perkins, Genpo Roshi, Chris Scofield, Barbara Senich, Robin Strongin, Beate Stych, Wendi Wasik, Danielle Volz, and Loretta Zolkowski. SEI generously allowed me to use one of their images. Stephanie Clark of Clark International Writing Services was not only encouraging but a superhero editor as well.

Others were generous cheerleaders whenever my enthusiasm flagged. Richard Vanderveer, who I've always admired for his innovations, comes to mind. So does Lois Arnold, who embraced ACTSage in earnest and used it to transform the lives of others. Two Guardian Nurses Health Care Advocates helped; Betty Long cheered me all the way through a presentation to women business owners, and Joanne Simone not only helped save my mom's life but became a fan of ACTSage and showed me new ways to apply it. Then, as I neared the end, Elena Brennan's CareCierge venture provided even more validation of these ideas.

I also want to thank you for reading this and ask that you'll be in touch to let me know about how it has impacted your life. Even as this book goes to press, other publications are under way, and your experiences can enrich those.

Thanks to my neighborhood Café 360 and all the crew there at Peet's Coffee, I'll be plenty alert during my very early mornings of writing and the long days ahead.

Last and certainly not least, I want to thank Robert Downey Jr., whose insights about pit crews started it all. Did I mention I like superheroes?

about The author

GLENNA CROOKS, PHD, IS an entrepreneur and innovator. She began her career in education, as one of the first of a new cadre of school psychologists who became change agents to improve education for children with special needs and talents. Her interdisciplinary doctoral studies and professional positions added public health, health care, public policy, law, and journalism to her expertise.

She was appointed by President Ronald Reagan to a position as senior health policy adviser at the US Department of Health and Human Services. Later, she led the global policy for Merck & Co., Inc. and became the global vice president of Merck's Vaccine Business.

As founder and CEO of Strategic Health Policy International, Inc., she solved tough health care problems for business and government clients globally. Called a "one-woman think tank," she earned recognition as a Disruptive Woman in Health Care for the innovative solutions she created.

Glenna was chairperson of the Orphan Products Board and the National Commission on Rare Diseases, founding vice chair of the Partnership for Prevention, and a member of the National Council of the Institute for Child Health and Human Development of the National Institutes of Health. She was also a member of the Pediatric Dengue Vaccine Initiative Board of Scientific Councilors and was a member of the Institute of Medicine committee advising the Department of Defense on bioterrorism and biowarfare countermeasures. She currently serves on the board of directors of the David A. Winston Health Policy Fellowship and Beyond Celiac.

She was the first civilian to receive the highest award for contributions to public health, the Surgeon General's Medallion from C. Everett Koop, and received the Congressional Exemplary Service Award for Orphan Products Development. She received the Samuel Gee Society Award for her contributions to celiac disease patient advocacy and was named a 2017 Woman to Watch by Disruptive Women in Health Care for her contributions to understanding Alzheimer's disease caregiving using NetworkSage principles.

Glenna is a fellow of the University of Pennsylvania Center for Neuroscience and Society, a fellow at the Drexel University Center for Population Health and Community Impact, and on the adjunct faculty in Health Policy of the University of the Sciences of Philadelphia. She is in demand as a keynote speaker and as confidential counsel to senior government, business, and patient advocacy leaders, who respect her for the wisdom and candor she offers about the dilemmas they face.

She is the author of several books, among them *Covenants: Inspiring the Soul of Healing*. Key chapters in that book, as well as other materials she has developed, are open-sourced available through a collective commons license on her personal website at www.glennacrooks.com.

Additional information, stories, and ACTSage tools are available at www.sagemylife.com.

The author is available for interviews, presentations, workshops, and mentoring and can be reached at Glenna@glennacrooks.com.

index

V

W

Y

Z